TOTAL EXPERIENCE CORNER

A Year in Jamaica

Christopher J. Cox

Contents

Prologue

It is 1988 and I am a forty-seven year old Head of Mathematics at a Comprehensive School in peaceful rural Somerset.

The slow burn fuse lit by James Callaghan's 'Great Debate' of 1977 has just detonated Kenneth Baker's Education Act. Amongst its many revolutionary ideas was 'The National Curriculum' which would stipulate what and when pupils would be taught each aspect of a subject. A year later the Maths Curriculum launched, along with a plan to ensure that teachers obeyed it by regular inspections and national tests. Many of the interesting maths topics that were introduced over the previous ten years disappeared into the ether and as I had just completed writing a major series of textbooks which included these I was not a happy bunny. After me devoting every waking moment for seven years to my textbook writing I then had to rewrite them to fit the new curriculum. Having just about completed this I felt in need of a complete change of scene; a sabbatical. But how to achieve it?

The answer came a year later in a letter from The League for the Exchange of Commonwealth Teachers posted on the staff notice board asking for volunteers to switch schools and roles with a foreign teacher for a year. My fiancée Gemma had fallen in love with India in the past and so needed little persuasion to accompany me if it was there that we were indeed able to spend the following year.

I applied and was interviewed. The interviewer felt that me teaching in India with no knowledge of any Indian languages was not a good idea and instead offered me Trinidad or Jamaica. Clearly she thought the locals there spoke English which, as I soon found out, most of them could but usually didn't, much preferring the local patois which even a year later I often could still not understand.

I had never been further west than Land's End. I knew that the Caribbean was somewhere off the coast of America, which was not so obvious to Columbus, but I had no idea where these particular islands were. No Google in those days but Jamaica seemed to be bigger than Trinidad on the map so, we plumped for there.

I persuaded The League that starting at Easter, rather than August as was the norm, would be better as it would give me an unbroken six weeks of summer holiday. Over the next year I completed the rewriting of my books and then much planning for the exchange was needed. A Jamaican teacher, David, was found, my second-in-the-department persuaded to fill my Head of Department role if it proved too much for David, an agreement made to allow each other to use our cars, and my house let for a year having found guest-house accommodation for him as The League assumed that he would not be able to look after an English house.

So in the early spring of 1991 much to everyone's surprise including my own, and having promised to write to my dear mum every day, Gemma and I, now husband and wife, left England for Duckenfield, Golden Grove, St Thomas Parish, Jamaica, and the adventure of a lifetime.

CHAPTER 1

Rule Britannia in the Blue Mountains

Friday 5th April 1991

Kingston Hostel for Young Ladies, Kingston, Jamaica.

Dear Mum,

Have you noticed that we are not at Golden Grove? The 'powers that be' have decided in their wisdom that we should stay in Kingston until Saturday – which is a nuisance as it gives us no time to settle in before I start teaching on Monday.

Yesterday's flight landed on time in the late afternoon and we left the cool of the plane for the shock of the oven that is the late afternoon in Kingston Airport, to be greeted with equal warmth at the foot of the steps by two young ladies, Miss Davis and Miss Jones from the Ministry of Education. Our luggage was then given priority offloading and we and it were whisked past serried ranks of custom officials at high speed and delivered safely by chauffeured vehicle to the Kingston Hostel for Young Ladies, the usual residents being away on their Easter holiday.

David, my exchange teacher, turned up here two hours later. He had been to the airport but had been given the wrong time for the landing. Somehow he managed to find out where we were and arrived in a twenty-year old VW 'beetle' (or 'bug' as they call it here), which he has bought for us to use. I think it will be an adventure. It has no wipers and no door locks, but does have low-profile racing tyres and ornamental fog lights. David assured us it was reliable but could not start it when he left and Miss Davis, Miss Jones, Gemma and I had to give him a push. How embarrassing for him.

The Bug - Day One

Yesterday we toured the Ministry of Education. I have never seen so many doing so little. ' Is Whitehall like this?' I wondered. They seemed very pleased to see us. I guess it made a break from reading the newspaper, listening to the radio, gossiping, or staring idly out of the window. I met the Maths Inspector and learnt that they have for some time been in the process of writing a National Curriculum. Oh No!! I am concerned about my school; the comments made were not encouraging.

No one had done anything towards actioning my work permit so we set off for the Ministry of Labour, being driven erratically through some of the worst and most dangerous streets in downtown Kingston. However the official in charge of such things refused to give me a permit, though we did not gather quite why.

The heat is enervating; 93 degrees Fahrenheit (34 Celsius) yesterday, with very high humidity and a water shortage too. The weather forecast is watched avidly by the folk at the hostel; I had thought that we might have left weather obsession behind in England.

New friends with Gemma

British High Commission

Friday Evening

Today Miss Davis, Miss Jones, Gemma and I visited the British High Commission in Upper Kingston, a grand building in well-kept grounds. We asked about driving licences. It seems that I am a rarity in being an exchange teacher with a car but after some discussion we were told that they thought that my UK licence was only valid for three months. However we could get a replacement Jamaican one from the Tax Office. So off we set off back to Lower Kingston where we joined a huge queue. Once we got to the head of it we were told we had joined the wrong queue and needed the one further across the room. Yet another queue, yet another error! Eventually, feeling like railway trucks must feel in a marshalling yard, we reached the official in charge of driving licences. He was not sure what I needed but consulted with several colleagues as to whether I needed a Jamaican licence, an international licence, or whether my UK licence was valid anyway. It seemed no-one had ever asked the question before but they would consult with their superiors and may have an answer tomorrow. We gave up and left. We shall have to take further advice.

Our next destination was a 'Kentucky Fried Chicken', where our driver joined us for lunch. Not the best of Jamaican high cuisine but it filled a hole.

We then set off on a beautiful drive north through Upper Kingston to Castleton where there is a large, pretty botanical garden. We saw many exotic plants, humming birds, butterflies, and a mongoose. We were told that the mongoose was imported from India in the 1800's to kill the rats that damaged the young sugar-cane plants and the yellow snake that made its home there. The snake, although quite large, is harmless to humans, as are all the Jamaican snakes, but terrified the slave cane-cutters who were more used to the often dangerous African variety. However as the mongoose multiplies as fast as rabbits and has no native enemies it is now a pest, eating any small mammals that cannot run fast enough, chickens, ground-nesting bird eggs, turtle eggs, bananas, and so on. Sometimes, or perhaps always, it is sensible to not interfere with the natural order of things.

We also had our first green-coconut drink from a machete-wielding Jamaican stall holder. Then we sat in the shade and suddenly the three Jamaicans began singing - gently and beautifully. We joined in with the songs we knew and ended with Rule Britannia and Land of Hope and Glory! Talk about a memory to savour. So spontaneous; rejoicing in the beauty of their island away from the city.

Tomorrow we go to Golden Grove and start the experience of life country style. As the city seems like the 1960's, I am expecting Golden Grove to be more like the 1900's.

Saturday 6th April 1991

And here I am. Nearly in Golden Grove but actually about a mile away at a place called Duckenfield.

Gemma is with me, but only just, as it has all been quite a shock, relieved slightly by her being able to find Ken Bruce on the BBC World Service.

We left Kingston at 10 a.m. The 'girls from the ministry' were early; all excited by their outing. The younger girl had never been to Golden Grove; it seems few city people have. So we drove the 40 miles along the coast; on our right the sea all shades of blue and green imaginable with the spectacular Blue Mountains soaring on our left.

Leaving civilisation behind we entered a world of coconut groves and fields of sugar cane until at last we reached a tiny, dirty, two-shop village, Golden Grove, or 'Grotty Grove' as Gemma renamed it.

Passing the school, set on a hillside surrounded by more coconuts and a view of sugar cane as far as the eye can see, we eventually reached the tiny settlement of Duckenfield, a cluster of wooden huts and wooden villas, one of which is to be our home for a year.

Golden Grove

Fortunately ours is an attractive small bungalow, optimistically named 'Royal View'. It sits in a garden of exotic plants, including bananas and mangoes and is the home of our widowed landlady, Mrs White.

We have two main rooms with a double bed, a table and two chairs, a small kitchen, and an indoor toilet (we gather this is a luxury item) and bath (cold tap only).

Gemma was horrified by the dirty kitchen which boasted two rusting gas rings on stands, a shallow sink with one tap (dripping) and a small cupboard. It hasn't been used for ages. Our Jamaicans, no doubt seeing the looks of horror on our faces, set off in search of David. It has improved now as once David was tracked down he brought a Calor gas stove with two rings and an oven containing a dead cockroach and several spiders.

Royal View

There is no electric point in the kitchen and no hot water system, so it is a kettle on the stove for all hot water - well it would be if we had a kettle. Something else for the ever-lengthening shopping list. I cannot expect Gemma to stay here without the vital necessities of a civilised life i.e. the ability to make tea.

Night fell quickly at around 6 p.m. All day we had the loud beat of reggae from a nearby hut but with the advance of night this was supplemented with much screeching and whistling, croaking and squealing. The insects in the garden were celebrating the dark.

Mum, you must be close to tears at what your son has got himself into although I guess we shall acclimatise even if it is all far more primitive than I imagined it would be. What on earth will school be like tomorrow?

Lots of love,

Christopher

12

CHAPTER 2

Cockroach Slaying

Monday 8th April 1991

6 p.m.

Well now I know!

Much brighter on both fronts today. We spent the most of Sunday cleaning up. It was all so filthy. Gemma worked on the bathroom and I tackled the kitchen. Once I had removed most of the grime I gave it a good spray of insecticide, shut the door for a couple of hours, and later shifted the bodies of a dozen or so huge orange cockroaches and assorted beetles. I do not normally mind picking up such things but the cockroaches are quite revolting and I have to use toilet paper to handle them.

The mosquitos are a pain; apparently this area of Jamaica is by far the worst because of the surrounding mangrove swamps.

I would hate you to think that all of Jamaica is like this. In Upper Kingston we saw palatial villas with expensive cars, swimming pools, huge satellite dishes, and a golf course.

Socially everyone has made us so welcome; Mrs White says 'Her home is our home'. She is well into her eighties and seems very kind. She was the local Social Worker so has a telephone, a privilege shared only by the police station, the school, and the Baptist Church pastor. She has lent us a kettle to put on the stove and an electric fan which may make the heat slightly more bearable.

Cockroach

We have also been told we could share with her the large ancient fridge-freezer in her separate kitchen. I opened it and was faced with a large pile of ice, food that had seen better days, and a quantity of chicken heads which Mrs White has explained are for her guard dog, Rex. I will try to tactfully suggest to Mrs White that we need to give her freezer a spring clean.

The wooden bungalow has a corrugated iron roof, or 'zinc' as they call it here, which only adds to the heat in the room. Yesterday we did a bit of basic food shopping at a small store in Golden Grove. The freezer was full of chicken feet, slightly less shocking than the aforementioned heads.

Cislyn in her kitchen

Mrs White has explained that these were what the many poor of the village use to make soup. We were spared this though, having an excellent meal with David's Seventh Day Adventist church friends yesterday evening and today lunch at the Golden Grove restaurant, which bears tolerable comparison with one in England.

We drink gallons of tea whilst the sweet juicy oranges and green-coconut milk make a refreshing change. Gemma amazed Mrs White's house-girl with her clothes-washing technique - she had never seen anyone washing clothes in hot water before.

We have spotted what looks like ivy stems on the inside walls but it turns out to be termite tunnels; there must be a nest in the attic space. Mrs White will have to get that dealt with before the roof comes tumbling down.

The spiders are incredible, some quite cuddly , some huge and hairy, some that seem all legs, and one variety as thin as paper that glide sideways across the wall like ice skaters, disappearing into the smallest of cracks.

The lizards are house pets and like much of the insect life

are our friends as they help to keep down the mosquito and cockroach population. I gather that what you really have to watch out for are the dangerous giant centipedes. These have a poisonous bite that can put you in hospital or even cause death.

School was different and needs a whole letter to itself. However I seem to have such a light timetable it hardly seems worth going in at all. I shall try to change that! David only has classes for ten hours a week whilst the rest of his department do twenty. How will he cope with the teaching load in England?

As we drove into Golden Grove on Saturday I saw a small roadside bar which was called 'Total Experience Corner'. I reckon we are due for a 'total experience' ourselves in the year that lies ahead!

Prepare for an avalanche of letters.

Lots of love,

Christopher

CHAPTER 3

I Love To Go a Wandering

During my year I was asked by The League to write a piece about my life here. It sets the scene for much of the year, so although it was written not long before I returned to the UK this seems to be the place to fit it in. The rest of this book is in chronological order

Five fifty-five a.m.

Dawn. The fan has cooled me sufficiently during the night for the alarm to wake me just as I lifted my lips to a spoonful of delicious strawberries and cream at an English church fete. Too bad!

I rise quickly. If I am not up by six the hyperactive Mrs White hammers on our door, concerned at the possible cause of my indolence. She has taken us to her warm Jamaican heart. We, and her, are the only 'whites' for miles around. Tourists never get to this very African backwoods of Jamaica so our white skin is a novelty and we have become used to the calls of 'Whitey' from the local kids as we drive past them. Although they must have seen white folk on TV we are possibly the only real ones they have ever seen.

A mug of tea is brewed then left to cool whilst I prepare our breakfast.; Gemma stays out of the kitchen until I have removed the bodies of the visitors who were tempted by our poison traps during the night.

The glorious flavour of the Jamaican fresh fruits and vege-tables is one of the welcome delights of living here. Today we have a grapefruit, huge, sweet, and so juicy, yet only five pence (UK) following the disastrous plunge of the Jamaican dollar. Very cheap to us but Mrs White is utterly horrified by me being apparently overcharged at the local market and on my return says "What did those cost you?" and when told says "HOW MUCH'!!?" Followed by "We're going back to the market to get you your money back"...but we never agree to do so as to us it all seems such a bargain.

I take a cold shower; a hot one is not an alternative but at least we have running water in the house not to mention an indoor loo even if the outflow does not get any further than a yard or two to the septic tank in the garden. Very few of my pupils have these 'luxuries' in this deprived depressed East-End of Jamaica, the loo usually being a plank-covered hole in the garden.

Jamaicans are nothing if not resourceful. Our neighbour living with his family in the sheds opposite is the cane-processing plant plumber. He discovered one day that the unused building next door to us, the 'taiter' (Patois for 'Theatre', closed since the English left in 1962) still had an unmetered water supply. He dug a trench across the road and so has free water piped into his abode rather than using the village stand-pipe. He also has free electricity by catapulting wires onto the overhead cables.

But I digress. It is time I set off for school. By seven-fifteen I am plodding along the road. One soon learns that a Jamaican plod is the only way to walk any distance in the Jamaican heat. The school is just a mile away and at this time in the morning the heat is just bearable.

Many of the school staff walk far further than I or travel in the solidly packed minibuses that charge around the narrow country lanes bouncing in and out of the myriad pot-holes like bucking broncos on amphetamines. The Jamaican national motto is 'Out of many, one people' and the tight packing of a Jamaican minibus does indeed make one continuous body out of many passengers!

View from the 'Taiter'

A few teachers ride a bicycle but on Jamaican pay none can afford a car or have any hope of ever affording one, so David having got hold of one for me, although it may be undoubtedly somewhat of a wreck, is a tribute to his kindness. However I rarely drive to school as the walk past the cane fields and the coconut groves, overshadowed by the heart-stopping beauty of the Blue Mountains, is therapeutic.

This morning Mr Spencer, 95, is as always up early. His beloved cattle family graze by the roadside, Red Poll bull, cow and calf, roped loosely together, a picture of bovine bliss. Mr Spencer is a true Jamaican gentleman of the old school and greets me with a doff of his hat. We exchange a few words (about the weather, what else?) as black clouds are gathering over the sea to the east. The climate is as much an obsession here as in the UK and no wonder when I observe the legacy of Hurricane Gilbert three years' ago in 1988.

It badly damaged so many of the villas of Duckenfield beyond repair leaving shattered remains, the dispossessed families living in shacks in their garden as they are unable to pay for refurbishment on a cane-cutter's wage of $31 (90 pence) a day. Even this is only paid in the cane cutting season from December to July.

International aid after Gilbert was generous and much appreciated but still only sufficed to provide new 'zinc' roofs for otherwise sound buildings or to build a simple wooden shack. The locals tell of much of the aid having 'disappeared' before it reached the intended victims of one of the worst storms Jamaica has ever experienced.

I arrive at the school gates in time to hear the first bell at seven forty-five and go to the office to sign in. I am number nineteen this morning and the other thirty-one staff will arrive over the next half-hour or so. Transport is unreliable and often late. Pupils will be drifting in for a couple of hours yet,

Today is Wednesday which always begins with 'Devotion', a whole school (or as much of the whole school that managed to make it on time) assembly. The pupils line up along the outside verandas of our two storey concrete buildings.

The vice-principal leads the devotion from the opposite block of buildings using an amplifier and a public address system, which works well when we are not suffering one of the frequent 'outages', rarely explained but making a hurricane lamp (how badly named is that!) or a candle and a box of matches vital in every room once night falls as it does every day at around 6 p.m.

The School

Gospel songs are sung, unaccompanied except by clapping. Some pupils, especially the girls, sing with much enthusiasm and obvious enjoyment. The boys seem reluctant to join in and stand sullenly or occupy themselves annoying each other. But those girls! Sometimes it is so moving I find tears streaming down my face. A belief in the life hereafter making the hardships of this life more bearable as it did in slavery days.

One of the hymns startles me, I had never realised that Crimond, 'The Lord's my shepherd, I'll not want' fits so perfectly to the tune of 'I love to go a wandering'. Try it!

The hymns are usually followed by a very long lecture on the need for good discipline in the school,. Wishful thinking I fear, and the words of wisdom fall upon stony ground as quite a few of the pupils either fidget or talk amongst themselves. Two vice-principals have been holding the fort for the past two months while their Ministry of Education in Kingston, only 40 miles away but on a different planet to us in this neglected parish holds up, for reasons inexplicable, the appointment of a new principal. The School Board did interview and made a recommendation six months ago but we are still waiting. The last principal was a retired Grammar School headmaster, now our close friend.|He took the job on for several years out of kindness but eventually could take no more and he resumed his retirement, preferring nurturing his small-holding to trying to run such a chaotic establishment. I hope my presence in the school was not the last straw!

Devotion closes with the raising of the Jamaican flag and the singing of the hymn-like National Anthem

Eternal Father, Bless our Land,
Guard us with thy mighty hand,
Keep us free from evil powers,
Be our light through countless hours,
To our leaders, great defender,
Grant true wisdom from above,
Justice, truth be ours forever,
Jamaica, land we love,
Jamaica, Jamaica, Jamaica, land we love
Teach us true respect for all,
Stir response to duty's call,
Strengthen us the weak to cherish,
Give us vision lest we perish,
Knowledge send us Heavenly Father,
Grant true wisdom from above,
Justice, truth be ours forever,
Jamaica, land we love,
Jamaica, Jamaica, Jamaica, land we love.

CHAPTER 4

Real Rain

The bell for first lesson rings on the dot of 8:15. The bell ringer is the most efficient thing in the school. An impressive quartz controlled battery back-up multi-function automated system. It is just unfortunate that only one bell is connected to it and that this is not loud enough to reach most classrooms in the school's four two-storey blocks.

I fight my way through the open corridor and up the concrete stairs to teach my top set fifteen-year-olds. There are 41 pupils on the register which is an average number for the older pupils, though the 11 year olds have a nominal 65 pupils per class with all four of the classes being taught in one large room.

Fortunately it is rare for more than three-quarters of a top set to attend school on any one day with closer to a third of the less able pupils making it. Many parents cannot afford the minibus fare, the textbooks needed, or the fee for lunch, although I suspect many parents assume their youngsters are at school when they do not get that far. In any case I have no idea how the school would cope if one day all the pupils on the roll turned up.

Today my Set Ten has twelve pupils waiting for me, although another twenty drift in during the one hour twenty minute lesson. Teaching here is even more than usually challenging as the school is never quiet and the glass-less windows on both sides, plus a missing door, do nothing to reduce the hubbub from other classes and the 'Anvil Chorus' of hammering and sawing as the metalwork and woodwork teachers in the rooms below mine instruct their pupils in the skills of welding and carpentry by repairing the many damaged tables and chairs.

There are rarely enough usable ones in any classroom so every lesson begins with pupils off on raiding parties in search of spares from a room that somehow has more chairs than pupils. On the very rare occasions when this is my room the disturbance caused by the pillagers from the less fortunate adds greatly to the general confusion.

Classroom

However today, fifteen minutes after the lesson was supposed to start, everyone has something to sit on, even if some chairs have only three legs. A bag of books suffices for a makeshift desk. The pupils are a pleasant bunch, noisy (aren't all Jamaicans?) but keen and eager to please. Like all my Jamaican pupils they like to have mathematical rules to follow and once they have learnt the rule will happily do hundreds of nearly identical 'sums'. I am determined to get them to think things out for themselves rather than just apply rules but it is an uphill battle.

Quite a few pupils have calculators, very expensive like all imported goods, but teaching aids are restricted to a blackboard. Textbooks are rented to the pupils through the UK sponsored Textbook Rental Scheme so most of the more able pupils have one. The school has been supplied with two computers but these are only for use of the office staff although as far as I can tell no one has yet learnt how to use them.

My next class is a nominal forty-two less-able fourteen year olds. I see them for four one and a half hour lessons a week and they are hard work. Today only twenty-six arrive. I suspect others are on the premises as all day pupils can be seen wandering around in the grounds. I dare not leave the ones I have just to search for the missing ones for fear of losing those that I have netted.

There is no text-book recommended for these pupils so I produce a duplicated 'Roneo' sheet for each lesson. The disciplining of this class is a skill I have yet to acquire, if I ever will, but today at least I manage to keep most of them in their seats doing the 'sums' I have written for them. I have tried the traditional punishment of keeping miscreants in during break-time but this can bring out the seemingly national trait of 'running away'. I have learnt to sit in the open doorway during 'detention' but even so on more than one occasion a detainee escaped through the open window. Running away to avoid trouble is often reported in The Gleaner, Jamaica's national daily. Uninjured drivers who have crashed and injured or killed people rarely remain on the scene. Even the police adopt the same routine when they have, all too frequently, shot someone. This week a ten-month-old baby was shot and killed, and a two-year-old injured, by police investigating a stolen video-recorder. The Gleaner reported 'The police left the scene in a hurry, refusing pleas to take the children to hospital.'

The dark clouds of early morning are now overhead and the classroom is gloomy. Once there were lights but now the tubes are missing. It is no matter as the light-switch has been vandalised and has its live terminals exposed. Most electrics in the school are in a similar state. Even the socket in the staff-room is bound up with insulating tape like a cartoon casualty.

A tropical storm breaks. It is quite unlike anything we have in the UK. I first experienced Jamaican rain soon after I came to the school and as the skies darkened I commented to the headmaster that I was glad that I had brought an umbrella. "An umbrella!" he exclaimed. "We don't get English rain. We get real rain in Jamaica!" How right he is. One rarely gets more than ten drops warning that the heavens are about to drop many gallons of water onto your head. If caught out in the village you may just have time to head for a nearby porch before you drown. Often accompanied by ferocious lightning and thunder (why do we always put those the wrong way round?) the torrent soon has the school awash. The rain pours off the roof as if we are trapped behind the Falls of Niagara. This hardly being a rare event each classroom block is protected with a wide deep concrete moat (Health and Safety would have something to say about that) which usually stops the downstairs rooms from flooding. When a fairly minor tropical storm is so dramatic one's imagination boggles at the thought of what it must have been like during Hurricane Gilbert. Those who did experience it still shudder at the memory.

As fast as it started the downpour stops. Just a few minutes later the sun is out and the humidity is rising. Just in time for lunch. It is only 11 a.m. but a sensible time when many staff and pupils will have left home before six. The canteen serves up a decent lunch though the menu is boringly predictable; chicken and rice or sometimes 'rice and peas' which is actually rice and red beans. With luck we also get a spoonful of shredded white cabbage or on an even luckier day a piece of green banana. Why do the Jamaicans, with a severe import/export balance, insist on a daily diet of rice which has to be imported when there is such a rich variety of tasty home-grown alternatives? At the local market we can buy corn (maize), plantain (a type of vegetable banana), green bananas, 'potato' (yam), 'Irish', (potato of the British variety), breadfruit and many other fruits and vegatables in their season.

During the lunch break the union rep. of the JTA (Jamaican

Teachers' Association) announces that there will be a meeting during lessons 5 and 6. School-time meetings are the norm here. Classes are set work and left to their own devices. This seems to work quite well as the pupils are so used to it. I set some work for my exam set and join the staff for the meeting. As much of the meeting is in patois I struggle to follow what it is about but understand enough to be aware that it is regarding the latest salary increase offer. This should have been settled six months before but the Ministry has been dragging its feet. I am amazed at the patient resignation of the teaching profession to the delay, particularly when they are so poorly paid and with inflation running at 60% and rising. The staff here are mainly female and about a fifth of them are what is known as 'pre-trained', which means they have come straight from being a pupil to being a teacher.

The latest pay offer is a 15% rise. After much noisy heated discussion this is unanimously rejected and strike action is on the cards. However with Jamaica millions of dollars in debt there is little real hope of an increased offer and previous strikes have soon fizzled out.

One more lesson until 2:30 then pupils are free to join in sports or clubs. I join the Debating Society, a small but keen group, mainly of girls. The National Debating competitions are very popular and David, my exchange teacher, has been highly successful training the pupils for inter-school debates in the past. Last year they were placed fourth in the All Jamaica Challenge Cup Finals. I am not sure that I am able to match David's knowledge and expertise but I will do my best.

School closes at 3:30. The weather is threatening again but I set off up the hill for home. Twenty minutes later a sodden creature greets my wife, strips off to get dry and cool down, then settles down to The Gleaner and a mug of tea. Gemma prepares a meal of traditional ackee and mackerel. I have grown very fond of ackee. When cooked it resembles scrambled eggs. The fruit when picked has a poisonous thread of red in it which has to be very carefully removed.

Mrs White, or Cislyn as we now call her, allows us to watch her television so we watch the 7 p.m. news (on JBC, the only channel) and by 9 p.m. I am back in dreamland. Now what did I do with that bowl of strawberries?

Love

Christopher

CHAPTER 5

Black and White

7th May 1991

Dear Mum

So what of life here. Well, we are getting used to the twenty-four hour heat, rarely under 32 degrees. Mosquitos are a big problem, though there are no Malaria carrying ones, but Dengue Fever is rife and can be nasty. We are not far from the mangrove swamps which edge the beach for miles and which as well as mosquitoes also harbour huge swarms of small black biting gnats, or the Jamaican equivalent. We have the cockroaches under better control thanks to frequent spraying, although I shall never learn to love them. I have become fond of the varieties of spider and the gecko lizards that pay us regular visits. We found that a Burmese cat was living wild amongst the banana plants in the garden and Gemma has adopted it. It did not take long to absorb the delights of living with humans: bowls of milk, fish, a cooling fan, and lots of cuddles.

The 'bug' (VW Beetle) is as much of a trouble as I feared it would be when I first saw it. We have looked into buying a different car but the price of anything decent makes this completely out of the question so we are concentrating on patching the old girl up. I have found out that the car had been bought by a local man. He planned to refurbish it but died before he got round to it and his widow sold it to David so that we would have transport of our own. I have managed to sort out the door locks so we can now secure it. The window-winder mechanisms defeated me but I have managed to convert them to slide down, held up with pieces of cane when we leave the car. I have had tubes fitted into the tyres as they went flat very quickly. Starting is still very erratic and I try to always leave the car facing downhill so that we can do a jump start if necessary.

However we have made a couple of trips to Post Antonio on the North Coast and stayed overnight at the Bonny View Hotel, set high up on the cliff with air-conditioned rooms and a fantastic view over the bay. Navy Island, once the home of Errol Flynn, is just off the coast. We took the ferry to it and took a photo of Errol's rowing boat, still bearing his name.

A Bonnie View

The entrance road to the hotel is up (and down!) a very steep 45 degree slope which is quite exciting. It also turns out to have been perilous in the extreme as when I took the car into the repair garage in the nearby town of Morant Bay to see if they could fit some windscreen wipers and possibly get the odometer (mileage gauge) and fuel gauge to work, the mechanic took a look at the brakes and announced 'You are not driving this car any further'. I did not tell him of our trips up and down the Bonnie View's mountain slope!

While this is all sorted out we will have to stay home. Gemma, having experienced the fifteen seater minibus, a converted van with benches and at least thirty people on board with the 'conductor' standing on the outside of the open door hanging onto the roof rack, pronounced "Never again!"

Gemma with Errol Flynn's Longboat

For a country of fewer than two million and not much bigger than Hampshire the accident rate is terrible. The road deaths for the first four months of 1991 total 129.

The police too kill someone most days. Usually they shoot suspects but today a schoolgirl was killed by a police land-rover. It is certainly a notoriously violent country though our St Thomas parish is fairly peaceful, the major problem being the locals stealing crops. The coconut farmers have threatened to hang 'scrumpers' and I am sure they will if they can catch them.

Cisyln is a very devout Baptist and we have joined her for the always very long Sunday Service. Audience participation in the sermon is the norm but whilst I might eventually be brave enough to join in the many "Praise the Lord's" I cannot see me taking an active role in the skipping and dancing during the hymns. The congregation, all in their Sunday best, certainly know how to liven up a service. One popular hymn is 'Lord send down the rain' which seems certain to prove God is listening because it does indeed rain nearly every day. Praying for rain, or for sun, reminds me of our rector at home when I was a choirboy. He regularly prayed for rain when we had a drought and prayed for sun when we had a flood. One felt sorry for God trying to keep up.

The sun shines every day too but we stay out of it as much as possible. We will never get a tan to match the locals anyway.

Cislyn thinks she is very posh being driven to the church, though the pastor has a Lada which he has kindly offered to lend me when I take my driving test. Yes, that was the eventual outcome of the research into the validity of my UK licence.

The youngsters seem to have become used to the sight of a white man and the pulling of the hairs on my arms to see if they are real is less of a problem although I think they were shocked when Gemma appeared at school one day. 'Glory be, there are white women too!'.

I am still struggling at school to tell one black face from another. With virtually identical hair there is not a lot to go on. The pupils have realised my difficulty and have fun pretending to be other than who they are. This is true also the other way round as we found out on our first trip to Morant Bay which has a white Roman Catholic priest of about my height and also with a beard. We were stopped by several locals to discuss spiritual matters. They took some convincing that I was not their priest. What they made of the woman holding my hand I would not like to surmise.

My more able pupils appreciate me being on time for lessons, actually marking their books and setting homework (well maybe they do not appreciate that), and their attendance and punctuality has improved. Things at school are generally as chaotic as ever and it seems some teachers regard their actual presence in the classroom during their lessons as not entirely necessary if there is something interesting to discuss with other teachers in the staff room. I am trying to set a good example but I expect they think I am an idiot.

I still have no work permit, not that this seems to concern anyone although as I am not being paid by the Jamaican Ministry I guess it does not matter. The usual arrangement is that exchange teachers will continue to receive their own salaries, although I soon became aware that David would not manage in the UK on his Jamaican one, whereas I was very comfortably off, so I made arrangements to pay him a share of mine, boosted by me not having to pay UK income tax on my salary as long as I stayed in Jamaica for more than 365 days. See you next year!

Love

Christopher

CHAPTER 6

Reggae and Snakes

8th May 1991

Dear Mum

We had a most welcome letter from from your grandson Robin today. It was good news as he writes that he hopes to join us for a holiday later in the year which will be a real treat. He will find plenty of scope to practice his photographic skill.

The locals are all very friendly although it is hard to see such poverty. Some go bare foot, whether of choice or lack of any shoes is unclear. Several women carry things on their heads, a traditional African way to transport items and no doubt carried on here since slavery days. This is not a skill either I or Gemma will be likely to acquire but I guess it could be fun to try as long as the object on our head is soft and unbreakable.

With such poor pay and a hard life the living conditions for many of the folk here, at least in in this part of Jamaica, do not seem to have improved very much if at all since slavery was abolished in the 1830's. They may have their freedom but they seem to have very little else.

The roads are littered with piles of fall-out from the lorries as they hit the pot-holes whilst taking the sugar cane to the processing plants. The sugar cane is set on fire before being harvested which pollutes the atmosphere but does help fertilize the field. I am told that this started because slaves were terrified of the snakes that made their home amongst the cane. The seven species of Jamaican snake are harmless, to humans anyway, but the slaves weren't taking any chances.

Head Carrying

Cane Truck

    The nearby shack-bars staged a Reggae concert yesterday night. Fortunately all that reached our bedroom was the deep bass from the huge pile of large loudspeaker cabinets so it was rather like sleeping next to the engine room of a cross-channel ferry, bearable once one gets used to it.

Cislyn, Gemma and Speakers

I have received a letter from Jen who is running the maths department in England while I am over here. It sounds as if David is settling in well. He has been invited to a Buckingham Palace Garden Party hosted by Princess Margaret. The League hope that he will meet her as well as be interviewed by the BBC. Jen's remarks about the U.K. Government's latest interference in the education system made me realise how good it is to be free to do my own thing in my own way. I don't think there is any real chance of the Jamaican Government interfering very much as it is safer to pretend schools and teachers do not exist. If they did realise that teachers are real live hungry people they might have to start paying them a decent wage. The teachers' salary scale finishes at the point a Jamaican nurse's starts.

With inflation last year at anything from 30% to 100%, depending on whether goods had to be imported or not, the 15% salary increase on offer was an insult. But not everything suffers from inflation. Last Sunday's Gleaner reported that our Jamaican Electricity Charges had fallen in the previous year, according to their numerically illiterate reporter, by 400%!

In some ways I admire the laid-back attitude of my colleagues here. My leaving the staffroom to teach my class when the bell goes is regarded with poorly disguised amusement. Then yesterday was the Year 11 mock examination which I was due to start at 8:30 a.m. At 8 a.m. I met their teacher. She was carrying a pile of typed stencils. I asked what they were and was told "The stencils for the examination. There are some mistakes, but nothing major!" as she headed off to the office. There one lady copes with the phone, visitors, the headmaster's needs, and the Roneo ink duplicating machine. I went off to the exam room ready for the 8:30 start and at 8:40 the first page of the exam papers arrived followed by the other pages at regular intervals during the next two hours. All was well. But of course!

David has one advantage over me in that he can at least understand what the other teachers and pupils are saying. I am still struggling with the patois, though I am getting there. Today my class were impressed when I wrote on the blackboard 'Gwan dis way' to explain the direction to extend the base line of a triangle to make an exterior angle. Some things are easier to understand than others. I soon got hold of "Me wanna rula."

So here we sit under our new high speed fan, the Burmese curled round our ankles, the tree frogs squeaking furiously, and Mrs White yelling as usual at her adopted grandchildren in the next room. What a picture of contentment we are. I have two hours forty minutes of teaching to do tomorrow.

How will I ever cope?

It's a hard life!

Love,

Christopher

CHAPTER 7

The Good Samaritan

Saturday 11th May 1991

Dear Mum

We now have the 'Bug' back from the Morant Bay repairer. She has had a major refit with replacement front wheel brake cylinders, new rear brake shoes and wheel bearings, front torsion springs, steering arm ball joint and suspension bracket. We also now have windscreen wipers and the speedometer works. The fuel gauge is still not working though. The total bill was £200 for parts and £45 for labour. As you can see from this, imported parts are expensive but labour is very cheap. We hope that we will now not be living quite so dangerously on the steep descent from Bonnie View.

I am sure that David could never have afforded the upkeep of a car on his salary. The Gleaner printed an article on teachers today and comments that no business would dare pay its employees the low wage teachers receive. It reckons 40% of trained teachers never start work, presumably finding much better paid employment elsewhere. Even experienced teachers are 'leaving the profession in droves for far better paid jobs'.

Mrs White was worried when she woke at 5:30 this morning because Rex, the garden guard dog, was missing. I realised that I had left the gates open when I put the car in yesterday night and feeling very guilty I crept out and shut them. Much to my relief I did not have to confess to my sin as at 7 a.m. Rex returned. Obviously she (yes I know she should be Regina not Rex) had come back in, although the gates were now shut. Maybe I was not to blame for her temporary absence.

Saturday is market day in Golden Grove so we took a ride there late morning and bought some fruit and veg and other items in the little supermarket. We had an excellent beef stew lunch in Daniel's Café, the oasis of clean cool gracious living in the midst of all the dirt and poverty surrounding it, and headed back here. Just before we reached our turning we passed a Jamaican Public Services (i.e. Electrics & Water) Land Rover with the driver standing in front of it. I called out "You OK?" to which the answer was "No." I stopped and he asked if I could give him a lift to Golden Grove as his vehicle had broken down. "Of course I can," I replied and turned the car round stopping in front of his to pick him up. Before I realised what was happening the Land Rover was being roped to my rear axle, the driver got back in his vehicle, and 'the lift' turned out to involve David's 20- year-old 'Bug' towing a Land Rover the mile to Golden Grove. Much to my surprise we made it to the Police Station, which seems to be the elephants' graveyard of broken-down vehicles.

The driver then went into hyper-drive, pumping my hand vigorously and grabbing everyone in sight to tell them of his rescue. He insisted on buying us a cold drink in the nearby bar to thank me, where he excitedly hugged both of us, taking our hands and telling all and sundry how wonderful the white English are. It's the first time I've been aware that us being white makes us somehow special. There was no stopping him. He recounted how all the black drivers had passed him by but "When I saw a white man coming I knew I would get help and I was right. Aren't the English wonderful and how could anyone in Jamaica say that white men don't like the blacks. I have been to Birmingham and I loved the white English and I hadn't wanted to come back here." We can understand that!

He would never stop praising us for what we had done for him and he would call into school whenever he passed to say hello. All this was interspersed with more hugs and handshakes. It was a cross between embarrassing, infuriating, and lovely. I assured him that he being black and me being white had nothing to do with it. He was a fellow motorist in trouble and I was able to help him. That was all there was to it.

We eventually extricated ourselves from the situation, but not before he told me he would "Call in and give me a cheque next time he passed." which I was about to try to dissuade him from doing this when it clicked that he was using the American expression 'giving me a check' meaning 'to make sure I was AOK'.

The Jhuns

This afternoon we took Raj & Naomi to Rocky Point beach where Gemma and I had a lovely swim in the warm blue water. We saw a guinea-fowl, a very strange bird with an impressively fat body covered in a beautiful pattern of black and white feathers.

A fisherman showed us his catch, a bucket full of multi-coloured fish including a pink one he called a snapper due to its vicious set of teeth. Again it was friendliness all round, except perhaps for the snapper. I hope that David is getting as warm a reception in our Somerset as we are here. England now seems like a dream and how strange we shall find it on our return to be back amongst white faces when for weeks on end here the only white faces we will see are our own.

Duckenfield

It is now Sunday morning. I rose early and strolled down to Duckenfield 'town centre', all of 100 yards of wooden shacks and bars. One of the shacks is a tailor's and as I passed he called out to me. A girl of about sixteen was leaning against his door-post with another doing some ironing at the back of the 'shop'. We shook hands; everybody around here shakes your hand when you meet, all very English!). He told me the girl at the door had seen me coming down the road and thought 'I looked nice' and would I like her to "Come and do things for you in your house." I wasn't quite sure what sort of things he had in mind, but I hope he meant housework. Maybe the idea of whites doing their own housework seemed unimaginable to those who had grown up in colonial days. I thanked him but assured him that my wife was quite happy doing things herself. On my return I asked Gemma how she fancied a house-girl to sleep at the foot of the bed but she apparently finds the lack of privacy here quite trying enough already!

We thought we would have a change today so after driving Mrs White to the Baptist Church we went to the Anglican one at Golden Grove. Today is Jamaican 'Mother's Day' and worshippers wear a small ribbon rosette, red if your mother is still on Earth and white if she is in heaven. The service was, well let's say Anglican Jamaican style. The archdeacon who took the service was half-an-hour late arriving so we filled in the time singing hymns, but not with the same enthusiasm of the Baptists. The service, once it started, seemed not quite right in the midst of bananas and coconuts under a blazing sun in a blue sky. The congregation were mainly old folk and it was not very inspiring. I decided that, at least while in Jamaica, I was a Baptist. Later Mrs White rubbed salt into the wound by telling us enthusiastically how absolutely, utterly, wonderful her service had been. "His preaching, Chris, it was like your spirit was lifted up to heaven. I thought, why Lord aren't the Coxes here to hear it. Ah, Lord, life is a mystery."

And so it is.

With love

Christopher

CHAPTER 8

Jock's Itch

3rd June 1991

Dear Mum

It is already June and time I wrote about Gemma's life while I am at school. She has been very busy making our rooms smarter and more homely. We now have some very pretty curtains, all hand sewn, so we have a little privacy at night. She has also cleaned up the bathroom, removed the flaking paint, and scrubbed the tiles back to their original pink.

We have also been to the up-town part of Jamaica's capital, Kingston, which impressed Gemma no end. The shops would not disgrace any English town. She had a lovely time trying on clothes and buying some too! We also visited a supermarket which would not be out of place on a British high street. It made us aware of how different things are in Upper Kingston when it is compared to our poverty stricken Duckenfield and Golden ('Grotty') Grove just 40 miles away.

Both of us are suffering in the never=ending heat so we are trying to get to an air-conditioned hotel for one or two evenings at the weekend, when we have a car that is, of which more, much more, shortly. My main problem is with 'Jock's Itch' which is brought on by being continually bathed in sweat all day at school. It is a problem for the locals here as well so it is easy to get lotions and powders which help.

We have met up with a lovely teacher couple who have been on Exchange for the school year in a primary school in Kingston. They will return home to England in August but we hope to meet them again before then. We met the British High Commissioner and his wife who have given us an open invitation to stay with them when we visit Kingston which will be good.

We have also invited David's mum to tea and been put in contact with another English couple who live on the south coast on the way to Kingston. Although most of the school staff keep themselves to themselves the Craft and Design teacher, Raj, and his wife Naomi, have invited us to their home several times and we get on very well. They are kindness personified and are both Guyanan by birth, with Indian forbears. When slavery was abolished in 1834 the expectation was that the slaves would continue to work for their previous owners but hardly surprisingly most refused to do that, so the plantation owners imported many Indian and Oriental workers, hence the big mix of races that now make up the Caribbean population.

The school has held an Open Day which was planned as an opportunity for the parents to meet the teachers but as far as I could see there wasn't a parent in sight, just youngsters having a Reggae party. The headmaster, who is leaving at the end of term, commented "I give up!" and I did not stay to 'enjoy' the music for too long either!

I have had a letter published in The Gleaner. Let's not be modest, it was 'Letter of the Day'! This is what I wrote:

As a UK exchange teacher residing in Jamaica for one year I am concerned that Jamaica, a Commonwealth country, looks so fixedly in the direction of the USA. Jamaica can never hope to attain the economic wealth of that vast country, and fly-weights should not enter the ring with heavy-weights. By importing so much from the States and always valuing the J$ against the US$, inflation is fuelled and a depressing, confidence shattering impression given to the people of Jamaica,

Surely Jamaica should be trading with other Caribbean countries and with the Commonwealth, thus stabilising prices and restoring confidence. Judged against the Pound Sterling, the devaluation of the Jamaican dollar has been about 9.5% for the past two months and *about 20% in the past year; serious, but not as shattering as the Jamaican dollar's 25% fall against the US$ in the past two months.*

Jamaica has great potential for growth but it can never be anything but a poor relation if it continues to regard itself as the as the unofficial 53rd State of the USA.

As a teacher I know from long experience that a lack of confidence and peer self-image are inexorably precursors of disruptive behaviour in schools. The same cause and effect are apparent in so many areas of Jamaica today.

I rest my case!

Your Christopher

CHAPTER 9

Horatio and I Are Taken For a Ride

5th June 19911

Dear Mum

    Sadly we have had our first bad experience in Jamaica and perhaps not surprisingly it involves 'the Bug'. We have named our steed 'Horatio' as like Admiral Nelson she it is missing quite a few useful parts.

    The bad experience is my fault I suppose as last week I noticed that one side of the rear of the car was further away from the ground than the other. I asked one of the staff at the Morant Bay Gas Station what he thought the problem was and he diagnosed a failed rear suspension. They had a mechanic, John, who would be able to fix it for me. It seems, at least in St Thomas parish, car repairs are carried out by private individuals not by garages. John would come to collect the car and bring it back repaired. True to his word John arrived at Duckenfield the same evening (I have no idea how he got here) and went off with the Bug, promising to return it in two days' time.

    I must admit I did wonder if I would ever see the car again and if I didn't what I was I going to say to David, but John brought it back at 5:30 a.m. three days later. He said he had replaced a wheel bearing and the cost was J$600 (£42). I couldn't see the car looked much different but paid him and then had to get John back to his home in Morant Bay. As I was still half asleep I let him drive. I was horrified at his speed. He was doing sixty mph. for much of the way when I rarely got the car up to forty. We took potholes as if his speed would enable us to fly over them. However we made it to his shack where he told me the car was burning oil and needed topping up but he had no oil himself. I said that I would sort it myself although I could not understand how the car had lost so much oil in the sixty miles maximum that it should have done since I last drove it. It had not been a problem for me when driving much further than that. Mind you I do not drive at 60 mph.

I set off for home and went to Golden Grove Gas Station to buy oil. I then noticed that the car had done 350 miles since I handed it over! The petrol gauge has not worked from when I first saw the car but I manage by keeping a record of the mileage plus a spare can of petrol under the hood/ bonnet (rear engine, remember?). It took ten gallons to fill it up again!

Then I spotted a rear tyre was flat – not surprising given the speed John charged at pot-holes. I fitted the spare, got a new tyre and tube fitted to the flat one, but then when I came to put it back on the car realised the cause of the problem that started this nightmare. One wheel was a different size to the other three! So that means buying a replacement wheel, hopefully from the Morant Bay scrapyard.

It was now clear that John had not done anything to the car except take her, plus I guess his pals, on a joy- ride around Jamaica. A salutary lesson learnt. Telling my tale to the Banana Company manager in the local cafe he has recommended a local man he uses who he has found utterly trustworthy. Time will tell.

Having little mechanical knowledge David had obviously thought the car was a good buy as the paintwork was good and it looked fine on the outside, but then so did the Trojan Horse and look what that led to.

Love

Christopher

CHAPTER 10

Report to the League

19th June 1991

The League for the Exchange if Commonwealth Teachers

Dear Patricia

Thanks for your most fascinating letter giving a blow-by-blow account of life at World Headquarters, LECT. You have done the impossible and made Jamaican bureaucracy seem completely sane!

The Kingston Ministry of Education phoned school yesterday to tell me that my Work Permit is ready and would I please go to The Ministry of Labour to collect it. I shall not rush in! As I have been without it for two and a half months I am sure it can wait a while longer especially as the journey will mean me driving the Bug through down-town Kingston, an area we have avoided since our first day here. Any trip with her is rather like a trans-Saharan expedition, requiring much careful planning and plenty of emergency provisions. Once I have a work permit I have to go to Immigration Control at the other end of Kingston to get my visa changed. My present permit only permits me to stay in Jamaica until April 13th. Now what is today's date? My arrest and deportation would seem to be somewhat delayed.

No major hilarious adventures to report, or maybe I am just getting immune to everything. We seem to have little reaction to mosquito bites now, although my efforts to cover drains in the garden and collect up the empty tins and bottles than made ideal mosquito breeding sites may also have helped reduce the menace.

The exam season is upon us. Jamaica seems to have taken the worst of the old British System and degenerated from there. I am quite horrified by the actual content of the maths they expect average pupils to tackle and by the wealth of misprints in the SCC paper issued by the Ministry of Education. Today I had to invigilate an 'Accounts' examination. The pages were seemingly printed at random, so the candidates had to read it in the page order 1, 6, 8, 7, 5, 2, 4, and 3. Perhaps it made it more interesting? I have had several long conversations with the officials here, but although they talk of change I am not hopeful.

The Baptist Church services continue to both inspire and amuse us. Last Sunday the lady leading the extempore prayers got into a highly emotional state and her voice became ever higher up the scale. Her "Dear Lord We Love You Sweet Jesus We Pray You Hear Us O Lord's...."'s grew ever more hysterical whilst the congregation did all they could to stem the flow with many "Yes Lords, Amens, Allelulias, Praise the Lord's..."'s until eventually the dear lady broke down into sobbing and the stormy waters of Lake Galilee became calm again. Both Gemma and I had to think very hard of something other than the reality of what we were experiencing for fear of breaking into a fit of the giggles, or possibly joining in the general hysteria. The prayer at last over we then sang 'Will Your Anchors Hold in the Storms of Life' which I remember my gran singing when I was a child (she only ever sang hymns, 'The Old Rugged Cross' being another favourite). Our dear prayer leader's anchor certainly had not held this Sunday morning!

David is snowballing us with letters and it sounds as if he is finding it quite difficult to cope with the many demands of an English school. He thinks he has a flare up of a stomach ulcer. However he has moved from the guest house to share the home of a fellow Caribbean from Grenada, so that might help settle him.

The good news is that I now do have a Jamaican Driving Licence. Taking a test seemed the safest option in the hope that my insurers would pay up if Horatio had an altercation with one of the too many erratic Jamaican drivers, although I will do all I can to avoid a claim as the insurance and car documents are still in the name of the deceased previous owner.

Getting the test set up was not the easiest thing to do and taking it took three trips to the driving test centre which is just outside Morant Bay so fortunately not too far away. The first time I set off for my test I borrowed the Baptist pastor's car, but after a long wait at the Centre it was concluded the examiner was not going to turn up that day. The second attempt, also using the pastor's car, was another failure as the office lady when I got there told me that rain was forecast and they did not do driving tests if it was raining. Fair do's I guess as the roads soon turn into rivers once the heavens open.

The third time I decided to use Horatio and we actually got going, only two and a half hours later than scheduled. The examiner complained about my driving all the way round. Faults included not stopping when entering the main road from a slip road; although there was no sign or white line I apparently was supposed to imagine them being there. Road signs are more or less non-existent anyway as the metal plates and the posts make excellent building materials when repairing a shack. Then I was asked to turn the car round at a minor road junction and did this by reversing into the minor road before I pulled out again onto the main road but apparently I should have turned into the minor road first then reversed out onto the main road! I was ever becoming more convinced that Horatio was going to have a very quiet life for the rest of my stay in Jamaica. My confidence that after 25 years driving experience with never an accident to my name I was as safe a driver as any in Jamaica evaporated. I was being made to feel that I was a liability behind the wheel.

We reached a roundabout (the first one I have seen and possibly the only one in Jamaica) and half-way round it I was instructed to stop and let the examiner get out! I thought that maybe he could bear my bad driving no longer and feared for his life. Not being too happy at stopping a car on a roundabout I drove off it and stopped when it seemed fairly safe to do so. The examiner then told me that apart from my failure to blast my horn at every junction, corner, passing car, whatever, my driving had been fine. He then left the car and told me to drive myself back to the Test Centre to collect my permit. Phew!!

Horatio is going to be put to the test herself over the summer holiday as we plan to spend about a month driving round the whole of Jamaica. I guess lots more adventures lie ahead.

Best wishes

Chris

CHAPTER 11

Life Saving

26th June 1991

Dear Mum

I have been putting my first aid training to good use.

Yesterday Gemma and I were walking down the hill towards school to visit Raj & Naomi when we were passed at high speed by a cyclist. When we got outside school we found a group of schoolchildren and assorted adults standing on the verge and staring across the road. The cyclist, perhaps inevitably given his speed and the state of the road, had come off his bike and was lying in a pool of blood. No one had gone to his aid but clearly he was in a lot of trouble so Gemma went into school to phone for an ambulance and I went to try to help him. He had a bad head wound which I put pressure on but he was unconscious, his breathing was erratic, and he was foaming at the mouth. I managed to get him into the recovery position and after five minutes or so he came round and in spite of my urging him to keep still struggled to his feet.

Another passer-by now came to help and I sent him into school to see whether an ambulance was indeed on its way. He returned to tell me that the only ambulance was on another call but the headmaster was prepared to take the casualty to the local clinic. So we loaded him into the back of the pick-up and as far as I know he lived to cycle another day. Lesson learnt? Probably not!

I have tried not to worry you too much about the dangers of driving around Jamaica and I do travel very sedately, even though I now know Horatio can speed along at sixty! There were three accidents last week.

On Tuesday one of my 11th Grade pupil stole a car. His driving skill was on a par with his mathematical ability it seems as he didn't make a corner on the way to Golden Grove and ended up nose first in a ditch by a cane field, completely wrecking the car but escaping with only bruises and a loss of 'respect' from his fellow pupils. This afternoon whilst in Morant Bay we heard of a crash along the Kingston road with an ensuing fire and five deaths. When we got back home Mrs White knew all about it and told us the driver was the man-friend of a teacher at school who used to lodge with Mrs White. She said he always drove like a lunatic and "He raced aeroplanes." We also passed a multi-vehicle accident on the way back from Kingston a few days ago. It involved a lorry, which had passed us on a blind bend a few miles before, and several cars. Lots of people seemed to be 'enjoying' the spectacle. I did not stop as there were apparently plenty of folk to help and I am never sure the starter will work once I have stopped. Horatio seems even less likely to behave herself after a long drive.

We too have been in an accident but compared to the above a very minor one. Today was the 'ground breaking' ceremony at school for the first of the planned twenty-five flats for teachers to be built in the school grounds A large display stand illustrates the architect's dream, including parking spaces for staff cars – somewhat of a sick joke given their low pay and that only two teachers have a car, the headmaster and me, and it is stretching reality a bit to include Horatio.

Anyway, only a few hours later than planned, the assorted dignitaries turned up; the managers for the banana and sugar processing plants, Ministry people, our Jamaican MP, two doctors from the local clinic, and a photographer from The Gleaner, all with their BMW's, Volvos, Granadas etc. parked incongruously smart and shiny beside the headmaster's pick-up and Horatio.

I don't know about it being ground breaking but it was very

nearly head-breaking as half-way through the ceremony one of the poles supporting the temporary gazebo that had been erected to shade the dignitaries from the heat of the sun fell over, bouncing off the photographer's head onto Gemma's and then, just to complete things, hit the side of my face and knocked my glasses off. Quite a pole dance. Fortunately there was no harm caused to man, woman, or spectacles, the pole being fairly light bamboo and so once it had been re-erected the event could be resumed with no further incidents.

Enough of accidents. We had a pleasant surprise meeting in the café with a girl from Leeds who has come over here for a month to sort out the affairs of her recently deceased grand-mother. This was her first visit to Jamaica and she is finding it hard going. She is living in her grandmother's house in Seaforth, a few miles away, where life is pretty basic. She has to wash her clothes in the nearby stream and go off into the undergrowth with a jug of water for her toilet. She seemed pleased to have an English couple to chat to but was amazed that we are staying for a whole year. Yet of course our living conditions are much superior to hers. It is the climate that makes things very diffi-cult but we know we cannot do anything about that. The best we can manage is to sit in a bath of cold water, though with the water pipe running above ground for much of the way to the bungalow, calling the water 'cold' is a bit of an exaggeration. However it is cooler than we are, so when it is time for our fantasy hour we take off our all our clothes (about three items between us), jump in, close our eyes, and pretend it is June in England and we are sitting in a puddle at Ascot. Lovely!!

Lots of Love

Your Christopher

CHAPTER 12

Legal at Last

7th July 1991

Dear Mum

We have been to Lower Kingston to pick up my work permit and get my passport regularised. They were pretty rude. I was told that I could have, or maybe should have, been deported for not having the work permit they would not, or could not, supply when we first arrived!

We called into the British High Commission and had tea with the High Commissioner and his wife; Both are lovely people. She and Gemma share their feelings about living here, though her]hardships are nothing like those that Gemma puts up with. She is shortly off to England ('back to civilisation' as she put it) for two weeks so is taking a pile of my book galleys to post on to John Murray. The High Commissioner knows of our fun with Horatio's erratic starter motor and offered to give me a push when we left! Disappointingly she started immediately so now the 'English exchange teacher gets a push start from British High Commissioner' feature in The Gleaner will have to be put on ice.

Gemma had a happy few hours in the malls of Upper Kingston but, as I keep reminding you, prices in Jamaica are very steep for anything imported. However she found a pair of red shoes in a sale for £7 so was well pleased. We just hope The Red Shoes do not have a life of their own, though she will be at little risk of being despatched by a train as the Jamaican railway system, from Kingston to Montego Bay has not functioned reliably, if at all, since colonial days,. Tthey keep on trying to get it sorted but 'going off the rails' is the usual outcome of their efforts.

That evening we went to our first drive-in movie. The sound comes through the car radio but Horatio's battery was not really up to a full length feature so at the end of the film it wasn't just the starter that wouldn't; the whole electrics system was dead. I guess that this is not a rare event as one of the attendants soon brought us some jump leads and a couple of girls in the next car kindly provided their amperes and dear Horatio's starter fired up first go. At least we again avoided the indignity of a push-start.

Last weekend we took a drive to the little hamlet of Bath, high up in the Blue Mountains in the north of St Thomas parish. As you might expect from its name, Bath boasts a spa, fed by very hot sulphurous water from a nearby spring which is three miles up a steep hill. Here there is a small hotel which no doubt was quite luxurious when Britain ruled the waves but now is very run down. However it is still offering bathing in the hot spring water which will, they promise, cure rheumatism, skin infections, and I suspect anything else one might be suffering from. An information sheet informs us of the many chemicals to be found in the water as well as 'Radio-activity (sic) in Cures per litre 4.9 x 10 – 10 and 0.9 x 10 – 10', which given our limited knowledge of thermonuclear activity may or may not leave us wishing we had never went! However I guess it is safe as it has been treating ailments since 1609 when a slave, wounded whilst attempting (or possibly succeeding) to escape his captivity, was miraculously healed after bathing in the spring. Thinking about it I guess he must have been recaptured and told of his wonderful discovery as the waters were made good use of from then onwards, though not no doubt by many slaves. The present hotel was built in 1747. It hasn't changed much since then so staying there must be for Spartans as there is none of the luxury we experience at our own favourite escape spot, The Bonnie View Hotel, Port Antonio.

We decided to risk immersing ourselves for the permitted half-hour in the hot water flowing into the bare concrete pools, followed by a cup of tea. I am not sure which did us the most good but it will be a novel place to bring any English visitors, swimwear optional.

Six English teachers are due out here in August and I have suggested to the Ministry that we have a day with them to help them understand what they are letting themselves in for. Mind you the schools in Upper Kingston and the more westerly parishes are reputed to be so much better than ours in the depths of Jamaica's East End. The idea of trying to help the exchangees to settle in seemed a bit of a novelty to the staff. I gather it has been usual to leave teachers at their accommodation and thereafter try to forget they exist. Anyway I think I have persuaded Miss Davis and Miss Jones to have a monthly meeting in Kingston with the new exchange teachers.

Whilst in the Ministry of Education I became aware that they were some way behind the times. In a world rapidly becoming computer orientated they are still using typewriters and carbon paper, with shelves of dusty files and ledgers looking like a stage set for a production of A Christmas Carol and only waiting for Scrooge and Bob Cratchit to appear, ink-pots and quill pens in hand.

We have been to the American owned offices of the Banana and Sugar Companies in Golden Grove and they are certainly up to date so the technology is there but I guess, like the sleeping computers at school, for the Ministry it is a case of 'If it ain't broke why fix it?'

It is sad that so many Jamaicans are unhappy with their life here. The Gleaner has just done a survey (they did not state how many residents they asked) reporting that 60% said they would much rather live somewhere else, most wishing they lived in the USA. Certainly many Jamaicans who can do so make their way there. The Gleaner has almost daily rants about everything that is perceived to be wrong with Jamaica. Much of it I fear I agree with.

Finally, whilst at The High Commission, we found a book, 'Queen Victoria's Secret Holiday in Jamaica' by Jonathan Louth which sends up her diaries and 1980's Jamaica. Do get hold of a copy. It is hilarious.

Love

Christopher

CHAPTER 13

Of Baby Mothers

9th July 1991

Dear Mum

I am writing this at 5:35 a.m. (Mrs White has a lot to answer for!) sitting on the cool veranda of Bonnie View under a duck-egg blue sky with fluffy grey clouds drifting by and enjoying the sea breeze and the view over the bay. The well-named Blue Mountains are just visible in the mist on my left. What a lovely change from the ever oppressive heat and humidity of Duckenfield. If we lived at 2000 feet in the hills instead of at sea level next to the mangrove swamps how different would be my feelings about this island. It is beautiful, there is no doubt about that.

We continue to try to get away every week-end, our hotel prices being eminently affordable as we get 'Jamaican rates'. That way we not only escape the heat but also the Reggae which continuously blares out from the shacks that serve as bars and food outlets. The 'music' starts on a Friday evening and goes on until Monday morning. Two dear old ladies run our nearest little store, selling everything from bread (the yellow 'corn' bread is delicious) and papers to brake fluid, though when I asked for a can of baked beans from a high up shelf at the rear of the shop I was advised that they had been there since 1962 and would probably not be a good buy.

Anyway, they find the incessant weekend drum-beats as trying as do we but no one seems able to do anything about it. I am told that none of the shacks have a licence to play records but the police turn a blind eye to it, possibly in return for a small fee, or some free drinks.

Duckenfield Shop

I guess for the locals the incessant pounding combined with much consumption of Red Stripe helps to blot out their problems.

Most of the Year 11 pupils have left school now so my work load is even lighter. I shall miss them, but when I asked one girl what she was going to do for a job she told me she was coming back to school as a teacher!

With the summer holiday just round the corner we have now booked a week in a chalet in Tortola, one of the British Virgin Islands. We shall take a local flight from Kingston. On our return we plan to test Horatio to the limit by circumnavigating Jamaica for a few weeks. I have done all I can to sort out Horatio's problems but she is a constant worry. OK, I know Horatio is a masculine name, but who cares!

Whilst on the topic of male and female perhaps now is

the time to write a little about the Jamaican families. The Pastor, he of the ever more hysterical Baptist Church sermons but away from the services the most placid Jamaican we have met, commented to me recently that there is something going badly wrong with the young men of Jamaica. He had noticed! "In all areas," he said, " girls are way ahead in exam results, responsibility, maturity etc."

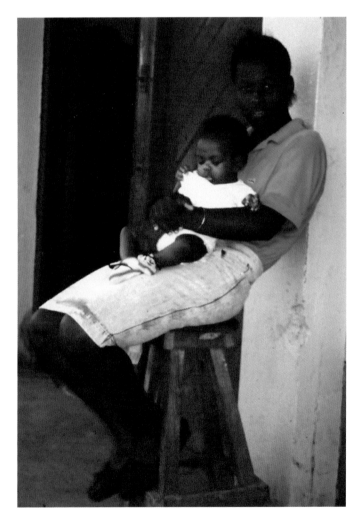

One feature is the many single 'baby-mothers'. Our white Kingston exchange teacher friend told me it was quite usual for Jamaican men to offer to give her a baby! Marriage is rare amongst the 'lower classes' and the men generally refuse to use condoms. I guess the women could use birth-control pills but no doubt these are expensive. Many Jamaican men, when their relationship leads to a pregnancy, do what Jamaican men do best and run off to find another willing female, never to be seen again. According to The Gleaner (again!) 80% of births are un-planned, though what evidence they have for this assertion is not clear, but given how many unmarried baby-mothers I see it is credible.

However if you are going to have a baby it is best if it is at least half white because the paler your skin the better the job you get. This was very apparent in the bank where all the female staff are half-caste or 'mulatto'.

On a even lighter note, last week I invigilated a Biology exam and looked through the papers afterwards. I much enjoyed finding the following gems:

On Hypertension:
Hypertension is a major problem in Jamaica because it makes people smoke.

Inheritance is a major factor in hypertension. This is caused by the discussion you will have to face with the rest of the family about what you have inherited.
Probably someone from the family wanted what you have inherited and so you get fed up and disgusted so you can't bother with the process you would have to go through so you can know that what you've inherited is rightly yours.

On trees in the desert(?!):
Trees grow tall in the desert because so many trees grow there they fight each other to reach the sunlight as there is too little sun in the desert. (Presumably someone got the jungle and the desert mixed up!)

On breathing:
You should you not breathe through your mouth because you could swallow too much air and suffocate.

What is the effect on the body of being a vegetarian?
Exhaustion due to carrying a lot of water to keep your plants alive.

Why you should not have plants in a bedroom:
Because you'll make it hot and tormented.

It harbours mosquitoes .

Plants blow the wind inside.

Insects can follow the plant and sting you whilst you are asleep.

Sleep well tonight!

Love

Christopher

CHAPTER 14

Bawling At the Sea

25th July 1991

Dear Mum

The summer holidays are here and we are just back from our week in the British Virgin Islands. It caters mainly for the yachting and cruiser-owning community so although we thoroughly enjoyed it we did find it extremely expensive.

Our villa was very plush and came complete with a maid. We had the whole beach to ourselves most times. We only went there in the late afternoon but were able to skinny dip, which is a much nicer feeling in the warm clear water than wearing bathing suits. We met a few visitors and enjoyed exchanging tales of our respective lives.

The flights were on time and comfortable, though the final leg was in a six-seater which landed in a field in Tortola. The only snag was that when we landed on the main island, San Juan, to change planes we had to pay a US$ 'security charge'. I only had Jamaican dollars and US$ traveller's cheques and found that neither one of these were acceptable to them. We headed for the Money Exchange Office but it was shut as it was a Saint's Day Holiday. Eventually we persuaded the official to accept Jamaican Dollars, but at the exchange rate of J$18 to US$1 when in Jamaica the rate is J$8 to US$1. We were being done, but better than having to fly back to Jamaica I guess!

Now we have a week to get ready for our round-the-island tour. Some good news of Horatio. The mechanic who was recommended to me by the Banana Company manager thinks he has found the problem with the starter motor – a fractured wire to one of the brushes, which explains why it was so erratic as sometimes the broken wire ends met, and sometimes they didn't! That will I hope be one less worry on our tour. The bill for the repair was (in English) £6. He said it had taken him 1½ hours to do the job. Good to know some Jamaicans do not cheat us, and a huge bargain compared to the £70 I had been quoted for a new motor.

On Sunday we drove up to Boston Bay, half-way to Port Antonio. The food shack there is well known for its jerked chicken, cooked over an open fire. Its reputation is well deserved, especially at £7 for two very generous portions of meat and 'rice & peas'. There was a white lady eating at the shack and we had a long chat to her about our experiences here. She had lived in Jamaica all her life but it wasn't until she left that the owner told us we had been chatting to Errol Flynn's daughter. You may recall he owned Navy Island at Port Antonio.

There is a 58% eclipse of the sun tomorrow which will be interesting, though a long way off the full eclipse to be experienced in Mexico. If we had learnt of the Mexican eclipse before we planned our holidays we might have made a trip there instead of Tortola as two of our fellow exchange teachers spent their Easter holiday there and found it interesting, even without an eclipse!

We have had a session with the six Jamaican teachers exchanging to the UK in August. I am trying to prepare them more than it seems David was for the cultural, financial and climatic shocks that lie ahead and perhaps help them avoid the unhappiness that David is experiencing. He is finding it difficult to manage on the grant and the share of my salary which I send him monthly and now wants to return to Jamaica at Christmas. Both of us signed a legal contract with considerable penalties if we break it other than for severe health problems so this is not a possibility and it is the last thing I desire. I gather that the League and the Ministry here have made the situation very clear to him but it is sad that he is finding it such a struggle.

One of the exchange teachers who is off to the UK in August is employed at a private girls' school in Upper Kingston. I visited there once and the difference to my Jamaican rural school could not have been more extreme. Quiet, hardworking, smartly dressed, polite, well spoken –and that was just the teachers! The girls all leapt to their feet when their teacher appeared at the classroom door with a polite "Good morning, Miss" then silence. If I had been placed there you would have received a very different set of letters but I would so have missed the daily dose of excitement at my school in the cane fields. Anyway I tell you this because the exchange teacher is going to an all-boy, multi-ethnic Secondary Modern School in Handsworth, a deprived area of Birmingham. She is going to have such a shock and how she will adapt goodness only knows.

The teacher coming here from Handsworth has exchanged before and has a baby to prove it! However it turns out that she thought she was going to stay in Kingston with the baby's father but, surprise, surprise, he has just told her that she cannot lodge with him as he now has a live-in girlfriend. Now who would have thought it?

On our return from Tortola we found that the whole of Kingston had shut down as Nelson Mandela is visiting. Our headmaster, who lives in the city, had offered to collect us if we phoned him when we landed but the shut-down seemed to have included the telephone system as the airport phones were also not working so we had to get a taxi. Of course the driver thought that we were tourists so quoted a charge of J$247. I have been here long enough to know that I was yet again being taken for a ride in more senses than one and after some negotiation we settled on J$100, still ridiculously dear but we could not walk the six miles along the causeway into Kingston, particularly with our cases.

On our return to Duckenfield the 'girls' at our local shop were delighted to tell us that the police had at last shut down the 'illegal' Reggae playing drinks shacks. I am not sure why but perhaps the backhanders were not forthcoming or maybe the

66

police have signed the pledge! We plan to take a month to go round the island and I fear we may return to find the shacks have re-opened but for now the weekends should be much quieter.

Another treat waiting for us in Duckenfield was to find Bonnie, Gemma's adopted cat, had produced three kittens while we were away. Obviously she is not the only cat in the neighbourhood! Mrs White thinks she can find friends who will give the kittens homes once they are weaned.

Mandela's visit has not been without its problems. The police shot at three people in the crowd at the Arena where Mandela was making a speech, wounding two and killing one. The paper did not explain why the victims were shot but the police can be very trigger happy so probably the offence was pretty minor. The Gleaner featured a cartoon of the police with the three victims telling Mandela "Well, you did say you felt at home here."

The Gleaner also reported that two of Mandela's bodyguards had been robbed at gun-point. One only lost his watch but the other his wallet together with all his personal possessions, passport etc. The rule here if you are threatened is 'Your money or your life' and this is quite literal, although often folk lose both; the bodyguards were lucky to have only lost their possessions.

You may remember me telling you of the Sugar Company plumber who lives with his family in the adapted garden sheds. He has two delightful daughters and unusually for around here they seem a stable family unit. The eldest, Camille, is ten years old and the youngest, Brenda, is four.

They have taken to coming into Mrs Whites and we have grown fond of them. Neither had ever been to the beach at Rocky Point. Of course with no transport it would have been a long walk, but apart from the few fishermen most Jamaicans never go to the beach. Raj tells us they are fearful of the water and hardly any of them can swim.

So one afternoon we took Mrs White and Brenda in Horatio to see the sea. Brenda, bless her, was terrified when she saw the ocean for the first time in her life and would not leave the safety of the car, but eventually I lifted her out and took her down to the water's edge on my shoulders, then gently put her down for a paddle. At first she clung onto my legs and screamed (or as they say around here 'Bawled') but slowly she began to calm and like a butterfly emerging from its cocoon loosened her grip on me and started splashing the water. When we got back to the car she pronounced "Brenda loves the sea!"

Our neighbours

I guess we shall take her again and possibly see if we can teach her and Camille to swim. Mrs White was able to buy some fish for very little when a fisherman brought his boat ashore. His catch was quite a sight; so many shapes and colours, purple, red, yellow, blue, green, white, striped, spotted.

Right, we are packed and ready for the off in the morning.

Love

Christopher

CHAPTER 15

Grand Round Island Tour

31st July 1991

Dear Mum

Your letter was waiting at our hotel in Ocho Rios. Some things work in Jamaica!

We nearly never set off as Bonnie disappeared on Sunday and I could not leave three kittens to starve, so on Monday morning I found an eye-treatment dropper and started playing nipples. Around 11 a.m. Bonnie returned; I guess she had forgotten she has kittens to feed but they soon reminded her and a bit later than planned we were able to set off for the north coast.

The bad news is that the starter is still playing up. Either the repair did not hold or the fault was not as diagnosed. Still, we shall manage all the time Jamaica has hills, of which it seems to have plenty. Your friend on holiday here is due to meet us here later and should have a VW Haynes Manual which may help with some of Horatio's little weaknesses which, besides the starter, include the tyres needing regular supplies of fresh air and the fuel feed sometimes suffering an air-lock. That is besides the non-working fuel gauge and the failed window winders (though my bamboo rods are doing the trick), etc. However I can still usually lock the car door though maybe getting it stolen and claiming on the insurance would not be such a bad idea! I'll try not to keep on about it but it is an ever present worry.

I arranged to phone your friend on our arrival in Ocho but the room does not have a telephone. It also does not have a plug for the cracked basin nor a curtain rail that does not fall down when you try to pull the curtains, but the air-conditioning works a treat thank goodness. When I politely, I thought, asked the recep tionist if I could use the reception phone one would have thought I had accused the hotel of having rats! "You'll have to pay for it!" she snarled. How dare a hotel guest want to use the phone! Basil Fawlty has a Jamaican twin. Anyway I got through and we are meeting up later. I decided not to complain about the missing plug!

We took a diversion on the way here, up and down a four mile hairpin road through Fern Valley which was pretty (and shady!). After the excitement of the hairpin bends we emerged to an English countryside with stone walls and rolling fields. The guide book promised a working farm there but it obviously had not attracted the few tourists in the area and it was working no longer, assuming it ever had.

Ocho itself is scruffy and dirty; lots of litter, piles of dirt, old breeze blocks and rusty 'zinc' . It had seen better days pre 1962. There is a tiny beach – well actually a sandpit set in a concrete pier. When we arrived we thought we could at least sit on the sand and did, but then the pier owner brought his dogs to defecate in front of us so we thought better of it and returned to the hotel. At least it was dog excrement, not human, though in our country area a human squatting by the roadside is not a rare sight. No wonder we often despair.

This is somewhat a tourist area so our white faces soon brought out the hasslers. Would we want a taxi, a restaurant, ganja (marijuana/cannabis)? At least Gemma was not asked if she wanted a baby!

Mentioning ganja, maybe I should address the drug problem here. No one in our village has offered it to me but marijuana is big business here, much of it illegally grown for export at high prices. However I know some of the pupils use it, a sure sign being head down on the desk (that is if they have one) slumbering peacefully. At first I used to try to wake them up as I would in England but the other pupils soon told me to leave them be and they would return to the real world in due course. Mrs White has a 'ganja' bush in her garden and makes herself ganja tea at night which eases the pain of her arthritis and helps her sleep (until 5 a.m. anyway).

Today the radio announced a new initiative to deal with Jamaica's multi-billion dollar debt to the World Bank. The initiative seems to consist of asking the bank to cancel the debt. If they do then no doubt Jamaica will very soon ask for yet another loan. It is sad when at the time it became an independent nation it was extremely prosperous, one of the richest of the Caribbean Islands, but now one of the poorest. Much of the blame can be laid at the feet of the long serving Prime Minister, Michael Manley, who through the 1970's alienated the USA by his support for Fidel Castro's communist Cuba. He even declared the USA ambassador 'persona non grata'. Without the vital support of the U.S.A. the economy collapsed and although relations improved once the opposition's Edward Seaga became the Prime Minister in the 80's it has never truly recovered.

Manley returned to power a few years ago with his communist leanings much reduced. You may remember that the Golden Grove banana and sugar operations have American owners and managers but I am told they might give up as it is so hard to make a profit here.

On the bright side we found a Chinese restaurant in Ocho and had a very good meal so we will sleep well tonight in our individual double beds in the cool of the air-conditioned room. Tomorrow we are going to visit the famous Dunne's River waterfall, more a cascade really but a big tourist destination where you climb up the cascade doing the conga. Then we shall head to Runaway Bay for our next hotel stop.

The adventure continues!

Lots of Love,

Christopher

CHAPTER 16

Christopher Columbus Was Here

6th August 1991

Dear Mum

Here we are in the middle of our stay at Runaway Bay, which is much nicer than Ocho Rios. This resort is very quiet and for much of the past three days we have had the hotel beach to ourselves with not a dog in sight! The big expensive hotels look busy but the small ones like ours seem to struggle to keep going.

Before we left Ocho Rios we visited Firefly, Noel Coward's house on a hill overlooking the bay. The site was originally owned by Sir Henry Morgan who was a notorious buccaneer. I will tell you more about him after we have been to Port Royal in Kingston Harbour. Noel's house was built in 1956. It is a lovely spot and one can see why he chose to live there in his final years, entertaining so many famous people, amongst them our Queen and her mother, Winston Churchill, Laurence Olivier, Sophia Loren, Dame Elizabeth Taylor, Sir Alec Guinness, Peter O'Toole, Richard Burton, and Noel's neighbours Errol Flynn (owener of Navy Island, Port Antonio), and Ian Fleming. The house is kept as it was when he died and he is still there under a marble slab in his garden with a statue of him gazing out over the bay.

At the foot of the hill up to Firefly is Ian Fleming's house, Golden Eye. It was not occupied but we peered through the windows! No signs of James Bond though, much to Gemma's disappointment!

The bad news is that our visit to Dunne River Falls was a bit of a disaster. I think I told you of the conga style tradition of climbing up through the cascade.

Unfortunately Gemma did not have suitable shoes on for such an activity and slipped, damaging her ankle. We had to cut our visit short and she hobbled back to the car. She was in a lot of pain so we headed for the hospital where they x-rayed her ankle, decided it was a bad bruise and sprain, bound it up and advised resting it for a few days. Thanks goodness it was no worse. It seems to be healing up quite well and is walkable on. We planned to take it easy here so it is no hardship to be resting for much of the day. We have plenty to read and a good view out over the bay from the shady veranda.

We celebrated our first wedding anniversary on the 4th with a lobster meal in the splendid Almond Tree Restaurant, part of The Hibiscus Lodge Hotel. Very upmarket but with prices to match. Our wedding date is the same as that of Britain's declaration that started our involvement in the First World War. No comment!

Yesterday we took a short drive to Columbus Park at Discovery Bay. Back in the fourteen hundreds the Portuguese had discovered the islands to the east of India, hence the term The East Indies, which is now called Indonesia. Although most folk are taught that Columbus discovered what is now the USA in fact he only reached the northern coast of South America and Central America, although he believed he had reached the Indies going the other way round, hence The West Indies.

On his first voyage in 1492 he only made landfall in the Bahamas and some other Caribbean Islands. He supposedly reached Jamaica's Discovery Bay in 1494 on his second voyage though not all accounts include this visit. He returned there, not entirely by choice, in 1503 after his ship suffered storm damage off Cuba and had to be beached. He was marooned in Jamaica (or some accounts say Cuba, perhaps he wasn't sure either) for a year. We know how he felt!

On his four voyages to this part of the world he lost nine

ships and never accepted that he was badly mistaken in thinking that he was exploring off the coast of China, in spite of evidence that he had not travelled anywhere near far enough round the globe by about ten thousand miles.

Horatio is still being an unpredictable naughty girl, so now I have the Haynes' Manual I have had yet another go identifying the problem with the starter which the manual says can often be caused by a faulty solenoid that triggers the cogs to engage. I took it off, cleaned it up and greased it and so far that seems to have done the trick. Fingers and much else crossed. The good news is that the brakes are working quite well! The road to here from Ocho was much better than any others we have used, no doubt because we are into the holiday hotels area. This of course means the locals can go berserk and, if that is conceivable, drive even faster than usual, so it is rather hair-raising. I keep to less than 40 mph and pull over to let the others get by whenever it is safe to do so, though most drivers pass us anyway, safe to do so or not!

You may remember we went to London before we left England to visit a London teacher with Jamaican roots who had exchanged to Jamaica a couple of years ago. She is having a holiday over here this fortnight with her mother but booked a 'surprise package' which means we have no idea where she is staying. However we sent her our hotel details which she should have received before she left the UK. We hope that she will get in touch so we can meet up. We have made contact with two of the new exchange teachers who we hope to meet in Mandeville when we get there on our way back 'home'.

12th August 1991

We have reached the outskirts of Montego Bay, a large town with an airport that delivers many tourists staying in the hotels here and on down the west coast. Our hotel is the best yet; excellent rooms with everything fully functioning and a good restaurant, plus a lovely clothes-optional private beach. We shall tan where we should be spanked. The grounds are fenced and patrolled and I can see that if the holidaymakers never leave the protected area, which they needn't, they will go home saying 'Jamaica is a lovely place.' That is unless they reflect quite why the perimeter needs armed guards.

Today we had to visit the bank in the city centre (Montego Bay 'city' has the fourth largest population in Jamaica) and we were back in the dirt and the rags and the hassling; rudeness in all its senses.

Yesterday evening we had a live Reggae concert at the hotel and, somewhat to our surprise, we much enjoyed it. Much better played live at a sensible volume in these pleasant surroundings than heard through the incessant thumping tower of speakers at Duckenfield.

Tomorrow we leave, somewhat reluctantly, for Negril.

Lots of Love

Christopher

CHAPTER 17

How Not To Make Tea

19th August 1991
Poinciana Hotel, Negril
Dear Mum

Here we are in the depths of tourist Jamaica but well aware of the upheaval in Moscow. We are very upset, as is I guess most of the free world.

Hurricane Bob is raging up the USA at the moment but at least it missed us. The other big news is that Natty Morgan, Jamaica's answer to Al Capone, is dead. The police have been trying to kill him since he escaped from prison just before we arrived in Jamaica and last night they succeeded. Courts seem rather superfluous here as the police, or local vigilantes, take matters into their own hands.

Dot, our visiting London teacher, has at last made contact. She is staying at a hotel further down the coast. We drove down to meet her and her mum and had a lovely evening. We have arranged for them to come to our hotel on Wednesday before they fly back to the UK on Thursday.

The mother asked me what I missed most being in Jamaica. Apart from friends and relations I had to admit most of the misses were good ones which include the rat race, the responsibilities, and the pressure. Given a reliable car, an air-conditioned home, a school with enough chairs and desks for every pupil to have one, then I think I would rather get to enjoy life here.   Mind you not if I had to manage on the appallngly low Jamaican teacher's salary.

Good news about Horatio! The starter has been fine for several days and I have cleaned out the fuel pump which has improved the smoothness of the engine.

The grounds of this hotel are very green and pleasant but the beach is short and narrow and no nude section which is a shame as we got rather used to being 'au naturel' on our Montego Bay hotel beach. There is no perimeter guard here and the locals hassle us terribly while we are on the beach, wanting us to give them some dollars or go on boat trips, fishing trips, tours of the island and so on. I find it very annoying. The hotel itself has its quirky features. There was a notice put up at breakfast this morning setting out what clothes was acceptable at the table. We hoped we were formal enough and were relieved when we were allowed to stay.

Last night's meal choice was lobster salad, ham salad, or chef salad. I asked if the chef was young and tender but my attempt at humour failed to amuse.

Tonight we went in and sat at a restaurant table, as one does. A waiter crossed the whole room to ask us if we wanted a meal. Well, yes, that is the usual reason for sitting at a restaurant table. When we satisfied his curiosity he then crossed the whole room again and came back to wipe off the place mats. Ditto to re-appear yet again with a cane-basket containing two knives and forks. Ditto and this time with two serviettes. Ditto to bring us two glasses. On his, as it turned out, final trip he brought us a jug of water. No doubt exhausted after this marathon he then disappeared and we never saw him again. After some interval we gave up hope of him re-appearing this side of breakfast so I attracted the attention of another waiter and managed to order our meal.

More fun in the morning! I asked for a cup of tea. Out came the waiter with a tea-pot and poured hot water into the cup. Then asked if I wanted milk in it.

"But this is just hot water. Where is the tea? You have not put any tea-bags in the pot."

"Tea bags?"

"Yes, tea bags!"

"Oh!"

And off he went with the teapot and returned with a tea-bag which he put in my cup of warm water, but no milk. I decided I would settle for black tea, but Gemma wasn't happy.

"What about me?"

So off he toddled and came back with milk and a tea bag, but no hot water. He put the tea-bag in her cup and threatened to pour the milk onto it.

"Stop! Where's the hot water?"

"You want hot water?"

"Yes, hot water."

"Oh!"

He picked up the milk jug and started off again.

"Stop! Please leave that."

"Leave the milk?"

"Yes! I like milk in my tea."

The waiter departs yet again and returns with the teapot of hot water. Gemma then gives the hapless waiter a culinary demonstration of how to make a cup of tea the English way. I haven't laughed so much for years!

Yet more hilarity at lunch with another short list of permitted clothes, different ones to the breakfast regulations. A male Italian guest was sent out for not wearing a shirt which was I suppose sort of understandable except that the side of the restaurant is open to the swimming pool with everyone in swimwear. But at least they *were* in swimwear, unlike our last hotel!

This afternoon I chatted to the social events organiser and found out that the hotel is entirely Jamaican owned and staffed which may explain the bureaucratic rules and notices. Not that notices are taken much notice of when they address the staff. This morning Gemma put the provided 'Do Not Disturb' sign on our room door while she washed and ironed her clothes. We hoped that this activity was not against the rules but did not want to be caught and get into trouble. However there was repeated knocking on the door which we eventually opened, only to be told by the young lady that we had to stop 'Not Being Disturbed' as she had to clean the room! A laugh a minute, or what!

21st August

Just back from a very different hotel, not far up the road but a huge complex with fences and guards. You could buy an 'All Day Everything Included' ticket. We were not completely sure what we were about to experience, though the name of the hotel rather gave the game away as it was called 'Hedonism'. I will spare your blushes, and ours, but let's just say it is dedicated to all the sins of the flesh your imagination may come up with. Clothes very much optional in most areas and non–stop entertainment throughout the day. It was fun and we especially enjoyed the large Jacuzzi; talk about bath with a friend! Everyone seemed to be having a great time and, sorry mum, but we may well come back for more later in the year!

Love

Christopher

CHAPTER 18

Horatio Is a Fast Woman

23rd August 1991

Dear Mum

We have turned the corner at the south-west 'land's end' of Jamaica and are making our way back along the south coast. This Treasure Beach Hotel is small and quiet with a lovely beach in the middle of nowhere. Yesterday our exchange teacher friends flew back to England as they had come here during the school summer holiday last year. We shall miss them. We had a great last day with them on the beach at Negril, swimming in the warm crystal-clear water and swapping tales of our adventures. We hope to meet up again in England as they live in Bristol.

Horatio's starter has been behaving perfectly since my last 'repair', but now we are doing the longer journeys it is not firing up reliably when the engine is hot. The manual says that this is a problem with the VW air-cooled rear engine even when the car is new and Horatio should by now be in a care home.

Confession time! No, not more about Hedonism. We invited our London friend & her mum back to our hotel on their last day in Jamaica and we drove down to pick them up. On the way down I spotted a couple of policemen on the side of the road but didn't take much notice. Coming back I got stuck behind a car in an even worse state than Horatio and decided to overtake it on a long wide straight bit of road only to have one of the policemen step into the road and wave at me to stop. By the time Horatio had stopped, sadly not her strongest point,

I was some way up the road but I reversed back to see what the policeman wanted. He did a perfect imitation of an English officer.

"Good morning, sir. You were doing forty and this is a thirty zone."

I couldn't believe dear old Horatio was about to be done for speeding in Jamaica. I thought that I was, save the car I just had overtaken, the slowest thing this side of Florida. I apologised very profusely and explained that I had speeded up to overtake another vehicle but had not observed any 30 mph sign. You may recall that when I took my driving test the road signs had to be imagined. This turned out to be just the same here. The policeman admitted that there weren't any signs but I was supposed to know that this was a build-up area. Well if wide green verges with the very occasional hotel entrance makes it built up then I suppose it was. Anyway after some discussion as to what I was doing in Jamaica driving a wreck of a car he let me off with a mild caution. I returned to Horatio........and of course although the starter worked she would not fire up! I contemplated asking the policemen to give me a push but thought better of it! However after I offered up prayers to whatever saint looks after embarrassed red-faced English drivers in Jamaica Horatio reluctantly got going and we drove on, even more sedately than normal.

The drive from Negril to Treasure Beach started out being quite difficult as we had a severe tropical storm which reduced visibility to virtually zero but, as usual, it soon passed. We drove for 2½ miles through a tunnel of bamboo which was very pretty then headed over the Santa Crus mountains. It was quite cool at the top. Fortunately Horatio seems to quite like crawling up steep hills in bottom gear. Near the top we were flagged down by some Jamaicans with a flat tyre. Their wheel brace had been pinched so they could not change it. I travel with kit for all emergencies so having carefully positioned Horatio facing downhill I took the tools back to them and we got their wheel changed. My lack of trust in Horatio's willingness to start when hot proved sensible as for the first time for a week the starter failed and we had to do a running start, a skill I have now perfected.

It is very windy here with huge breakers rolling in, so different to our time at Negril, but it is the hurricane season so maybe we should not be surprised.

Talking of hurricanes, I stormed out of a bank in Negril when they would not cash a cheque without me paying them J $20 so that they could phone my Morant Bay bank to check it was OK to give me my money. I went to a different bank where they cashed the cheque with no problem. Of course it all took ages. Banking is a very slow process here and it is nothing to be in the building for over an hour. They usually have a TV rigged up to help pass the time. No cash points of course, just lots of bureaucracy and much paper work.

Oh look, a flock of pelicans are just flying over.

What a wonderful bird is the pelican....

Lots of love

Your speeding son

Christopher

Photo by kind permission of Circe Denyer

CHAPTER 19

The Gut Buster

31st August 1991

Dear Mum

Safely back in Duckenfield. Our last week was very relaxing. We met two new exchange teachers from Bath (England) and got on well with them, although as they are a five-hour drive from here and do not have a car themselves I doubt we shall see much of them but will keep in touch by phone. Back in Kingston we rounded things off with a night at the British High Commission. In the morning we were told the last people to have slept in the beds we used were Margaret and Dennis Thatcher! Maybe it was just as well they told us in the morning or I may not have slept as well as I did.

Gemma's Canadian Aunt and Uncle escape the winter cold by renting an apartment in Destin on the Florida coast and we have been invited to spend our Christmas holiday with them, so whilst in Kingston we booked our Florida flight and also managed to confirm our air tickets back to the UK. That pleased Gemma no end!

The drive back here was uneventful, which made a nice change. Lots of letters were waiting to be opened including several from David who is still very unhappy with his financial situation in the UK. Unfortunately he will find his finances much worse when he returns as the Jamaican dollar continues to fall in value. It was J$15 to the £1 when we came, now four months later it is J$20. As teachers have still had not had the 15% pay rise offered in April David will find his income down by over 30%, from J$145 to J$96 a month. Flour went up by 30% yesterday so today bread has increased by the same amount. The Island's nurses have been on strike for a week to try to get a pay rise, although they are better off than the teachers. State teachers' pay is from £1200 to £2400 a year, whilst nurses get from £2400 to £6000.

I was pleased to learn that I shall no longer be the only white face in the school as a USA Peace Core (equivalent to VSO in the UK) volunteer, Robert, is to join the staff to teach mathematics. We met him briefly as he came to Mrs White to try to sort out some accommodation, which he succeeded in doing and he will lodge with a friend of hers along the road to school. We got on well and I look forward to his company at school.

The Gutbuster

I don't think I have told you about our local ice-cream shack, 'The Gut Buster'. Once a fortnight they get a delivery and we have a standing order for a large tub of their excellent Crazy Jim vanilla which keeps well in Mrs White's freezer. When I went to pick up my luxury item yesterday I found a new Reggae shack had opened up and the tower of speakers were doing their worst. It was painful on the ears to walk past them.

Awaiting me on my return was yet another letter from David, this time informing me that a family of Jamaican ancestry who he has been in contact with in the UK are coming to Jamaica for a holiday next week and please would I let them have use of the car. It is only for three weeks so I guess I can manage without it. What they will make of it I do not know as I think David has not told them of Horatio's fragile constitution.

12th September 1991

I did not get very far into the new school year before I went down with a very high temperature and a swollen painful neck so I have had to take some time off. Gemma thinks I have 'schoolitis' and certainly it has got off to a tragic start as one of my Year Eight girls was brutally murdered along with her mother at the weekend. The father is OK and says it was the result of five robbers breaking in and killing his wife and his step-daughter when they tried to drive the robbers out of the house. He escaped by running away. Although a murder during a robbery is all too common in Jamaica I somehow wonder if his story is not rather fanciful and it was in fact a domestic incident.

If this had happened to a pupil in Somerset the whole school would have gone into shock but here the staff and pupils seem not too surprised or upset though they did collect for a wreath. To add to the local woes another man was robbed and shot dead in Morant Bay a week ago. Yesterday we went to the bank there and the town was full of the Jamaican Special Squad, all two of them. Today The Gleaner reports that a man has been arrested but not, for once, shot.

I did wonder when I first arrived why the locals do not

grow their own produce. There seems plenty of ground available but of course I now realise that anything they did grow would be stolen. The Gleaner had an article about an old lady farmer who shoots at anyone seen approaching her land. The writer seems to think she is doing a good job. Another farmer boasts that he shoots, as if they were pigeons, anyone seen up his coconut trees!

Today sees the third anniversary of Hurricane Gilbert. Fortunately so far this year the Caribbean has been spared and the only hurricane to have touched any land at all was Bob in North Carolina; however it is still only the middle of the season which runs from June to November. It has though been a very hot year, often reaching 38°C but by December it should be down, often dropping to around thirty. I might need my thermal vest yet.

Cislyn can yarn for Jamaica and her tales have more blind alleys than a maze, but she never loses sight of the target and unfailingly returns confidently from a digression to exactly where she left the main story which eventually reaches its conclusion. She entertains me for hours. One of her favourite tales is the miracle of the baby during Gilbert. Apparently a villa up the road had its roof smashed in by a falling coconut tree, hitting the room where a baby was in its cot. When the panic stricken mother went to see what was left of her offspring she found the baby surrounded by coconuts but none had hit him. "Now that truly was a miracle." said Cislyn.

She took refuge, with most of the village, at the school and was lucky as her villa only suffered the loss of some sheets of zinc from the roof. Maybe not so much down to luck as to the good building skills of her husband. The villa opposite is completely wrecked though someone still lives in the one patched-up room.

School has its own hurricane to contend with as the deputy head has taken over until, or if, a new head-teacher is appointed by the Ministry. Mind you she is convinced that she will be given the job and is therefore doing her best to sort out the school's many problems. She has set up powerful loudspeakers over which she yells at pupils (and teachers) who are not in their classrooms when they should be. It is so loud that I cannot compete and have to stop talking until she has finished. One gem today was "That boy just going into the girls' toilets. Stop! Stop!! Come Here!"

She has also completely re-organised the school day, moving, at my suggestion, registration to half-way through the day when there is a better chance that all, or at least most, of the pupils (and teachers) will have made it on site. Unfortunately today she forgot the changed times and announced lunch break twenty minutes too early. Everyone left their classrooms. She then realised her mistake and followed it up in a panic with "That was wrong! Go back to your lessons! Go back! Go! Now!" This had limited effect!

Although I admire her efforts I do not hold out a lot of hope. It was apparent during the many long staff meetings before the pupils returned that many of the staff are not happy with her appointment which will make things difficult for her. She eventually sorted out the new timetable and I am pleased to be again teaching the top classes in Years 10 and 11. The Year 11 class cheered when I turned up to take their first lesson. I think that was a good sign!

Robert, Peace Core volunteer, is more and more amazed at what goes on and I love watching his face as he observes our funny little ways. He told me he thinks the whole place is mad. Fancy that!

Robert gave us all a fright at lunch the other day when he suddenly went bright red, gasped for air and fell to the floor. Either by accident or design his chicken, rice and peas, normally bland, had a whole Jamaican 'Granny's chilli in it. These are the hottest chilli bar none and he had taken a large bite into it. Several glasses of water later he recovered. He will be more cautious in future that is for sure.

Brenda, Robert and Gemma

As I mentioned earlier, David's friend turned up and I let him take Horatio. Two days later he returned her! He told me she was no good and he was going to hire a car for the rest of his stay. That is fine with me, especially now that I have found out what had gone wrong this time. It took me all of five minutes to sort it out! It seems that when I had new spark plugs fitted before our island tour the mechanic must have not done up the spark plug connectors tight enough and two of the leads had unscrewed and fallen off. The game girl had motored back to Duckenfield on two cylinders! I wonder how many modern cars would manage to keep going with half their engine not operating! Someone up there was looking after me as she could have thrown off her leads at anytime since July but chose just the right moment so that she could return to her loving Chris. Perhaps Cislyn has been praying as I know she was not looking forward to three weeks of walking up the hill to church.

Now I have a car I took Mrs White's gas cylinders into Morant Bay for refilling. The usual place had run out so I tried another but was told my empty cylinders were the wrong colour. They are painted cream but should be silver, so they refused to fill them. I ask you! I shall have to go to my usual supplier another day.

14th September

I have shaken off the bug and returned to school, though now Gemma has caught it; nowhere near as badly as me of course. but then I had man 'flu.

While I have been on my death bed at home the stand-in deputy head has elevated her position and is now to be known as 'The Principal'. She has decided that pupils must not pass her room or the school office or the Bursar's room or the staff-room. I gather that at first she brought in breeze blocks to make a wall at each end of the forbidden area but that stopped 'legitimate' visitors, not to mention the teachers, reaching their staffroom, so that did not last long. Instead she has now found a can of red paint and in large letters at each end of the banned area has painted on the concrete corridor floor 'Pupils are not to pass this point'. It reminds me of the regulations posted in the hotel in Negril. For now the pupils are obeying but they have to make quite a long detour round the waste ground at the rear of the school to get to the library and the classrooms on the other side of the sacred ground.

Brenda is a daily visitor to Royal View and I have suggested that Gemma tries to teach her to read. She is a nice kid but will not get out of the poverty trap if she is unable to read and write. We must start our swimming lessons for her and her sister now we are back.

Just to round things off can I share some advice from The Gleaner on dealing with the slug menace. Yes, they are a problem over here too. There are four methods advised. (1) The snip and slice method. Go out at night with a lantern and scissors and snip the slugs in half. (2) Crush the slugs to death by stomping on them with large boots. (3) Trap them under boards then dispose of them by either method 1 or 2 at your choice. (4) Drown them in Red Stripe; this is kinder as they at least die happy.

Lots of Love

Christopher

Brenda at Home

Gemma at Brenda's Home

CHAPTER 20

Of Mice and Men

15th September 1991

Dear Mum

A grey, rainy, colder (well let's say cooler) Sunday afternoon. I am not hallucinating and we are still in Jamaica. We are in the middle of what is termed a Tropical Wave and we are lucky that it did not turn into a hurricane. We have had some impressive storms with lightning, thunder and torrential rain, not continuous but in bursts of ten to twenty minutes. The garden is now a shallow lake and there is a flash flooding alert for the whole of Jamaica. The TV is off the air and the power outages a daily event. We hope that the weather improves by the time Robin gets here for his three week holiday at the end of October.

As there is not much else to report I have collected together a few odd bits for you.

School

I am still finding my bottom Year 9 set nearly impossible to control but I keep up the good fight. There are officially 34 of them but rarely more than 15 turn up on any one day. With the changes to the school day the electronic bell system was ringing at all the wrong times and none of the other staff knew how to alter it, but I sorted it for them. I am now waiting to be asked to set the two computers up for them. Or not!

Mice

We have a family of mice in our kitchen. I caught one yesterday but could not bear to kill it so took it into the garden.

When I got back to the kitchen there was another one (or possibly it was the same one) whiskering about and I was unable to catch it before it bolted through a hole in the wall. We have a cat and three kittens, and still we have mice.

Robert

Robert's mentor called in this week to see how he is getting on at school. He brought him a new mountain bike which I think is asking for trouble as it would cost a year's pay to a cane cutter. Already one of the vice-principals has asked Robert to give it to her when he leaves in two years' time. Will he still have it by then? She cannot have it anyway as it is only on loan.

Horatio

I keep tinkering with Horatio who continues to be very unpredictable, but so far we have always got to where we intended and made it back again which I guess is what counts. Really she needs a new battery, distributor, starter, fuel pump, carburettor, engine, gear box, steering, chassis and body! The steering and the clutch seem OK!

Morant Bay priest

We continue having locals seek spiritual guidance from me when we go into Morant Bay, but we have now met Father Austin and can see why there is confusion as we do look quite similar and as he hails from Bristol he has a West Country accent to boot.

Pupils' names

Some of the pupils have rather strange names. I know you are Florence, but I have a Venice in one of my classes, as well as a Novelette and a boy called Devon. Haven't met a Somerset or even a Dorset yet though.

Prices

With the fall in the Jamaican dollar the prices of the many imported goods are bound to rise. Petrol, which was J$16 back in April is now J$26. A loaf of bread now costs J$10 and as a cane cutter earns J$31 a day I have noticed in our local shop people asking for a quarter of a loaf, one cigarette, or just two eggs. The Prime Minister was asked about this on TV and had the nerve to comment that if the poor could not afford to buy a large loaf then the bakers had better bake smaller ones. It reminded me of Marie Antoinette and it is not entirely impossible that he could end up with the same untimely end though not by guillotining I guess. The problem, as ever, is too few exports and too many imports, but Jamaica has no oil wells, cannot grow wheat or rice, and has no home-built technology. It does have a huge reserve of bauxite from which aluminium is made but is struggling to compete with other bauxite producing countries and does not profit as it should as the marketing is done by large international companies.

The Police

The Gleaner reported that the police had shot and killed a driver who did not stop at a check point. Good job then that I stopped in Negril even if stopping is not Horatio's strong point. Come to think of it starting is not her strong point either!

All for now

Love

Christopher

CHAPTER 21

Mirror on the Ceiling

25th September 1991

Dear Mum

Thanks for your letter and the box of purification tablets. They seem unobtainable in Jamaica though I have been advised that two drops of bleach in a quart of water does the trick. I am not sure about that. To start with, how big is a drop?

Inflation gets worse by the day. Our UK sterling exchange rate cancels it out for us but not for Jamaicans; they have seen their dollar go from 15 to the £1 sterling to 23. The government has now taken off all exchange controls and the NCB bank is today quoting J$27 to £1. When we first came here we multiplied a Jamaican dollar price by seven to get a comparison with sterling; now we multiply by four so for us things seem to be getting cheaper. I have had a pair of trousers made by the Duckenfield tailor at a cost of J$70 for labour and J$50 for the cloth, a grand total in sterling of less than £5. He made a great job of it too.

Horatio's electrics continue to be a problem. I have found a bad connection between the distributor and the coil and sorting this out seems to have improved things for now.

We have been looking for things for Robin to do when he comes. There is a two-day tour of Jamaica on offer. Also a bike ride down the Blue Mountains, 'Truck up, free-wheel down'; I don't think I shall mention that to him. There are places we have not visited ourselves but as his visit does not coincide with half-term as we initially hoped we shall have to leave him to explore on his own for some of the time. The acting head keeps altering the timetable and I now have only one lesson on a Wednesday, right in the middle of the day. To balance this I have no time off on Thursday and Friday. I guess while Robin is here I could just not turn up some days, which other teachers seem to do but I am trying to set a good example.

I have sent off some films of our Round Jamaica Tour for you to have developed for us please. Nothing too shocking I hope as I refrained from taking photos on the nudist beaches. However you will find that there is one from Hedonism of a bedroom with a mirror on the ceiling above the bed. That seems a very silly place to put a mirror and must make shaving difficult.

A friend of Raj has just brought us a huge bunch of green bananas, apparently 'rejects', or maybe not. Whatever, they take about a month to ripen and then we have too many. We can cook the green ones though the larger type, called plantain, are better for that and when ripe make a good fried breakfast. For some reason bananas in the market are in short supply which is quite puzzling. However avocados are plentiful and very good, as is the ackee. The mango seasons seems to be over now.

10th October

The heat is less oppressive, rarely above 90°F (32°C). Incredibly some of the pupils now wear woolly jumpers as they find it chilly! We also are suffering lots of heavy rainstorms creating mini-ponds which must delight the mosquitoes. Mrs White has taken a lodger, a security guard at the banana plantation. He tells me that he is unarmed and his guard post is apparently over a mile from the next one with no communication when he is on duty. If he found banana thieves and they turned nasty he has one master plan viz. to run away as fast as possible. Just after he told me this I read in the Gleaner that a security guard at the prestigious Devon House in Kingston was killed by having his throat cut during a robbery. Maybe it is understandable why the police shoot first and ask questions

19th October

Robin has arrived and we are so happy to have him with us. We nearly did not make it to the airport as Horatio chose our drive through the mountains to the airport to suffer a blocked fuel pipe. However with much huffing and puffing I got it clear and anyway as it turned out the plane was an hour late landing. We saw it land but two hours later there was still no sign of Robin so we thought he must have missed it. Much to our relief he eventually arrived, explaining that his case was last off the plane and the queue to get through customs was enormous and very slow moving, but this is Jamaica after all. I have become used to the simplest tasks taking half the day. Why worry! Be happy!

29th October

It was Robin's birthday on the 24th so we took him into the Blue Mountains to a coffee plantation. The plan was to have lunch at an upmarket restaurant there but it was closed so Robin had to settle for corned beef sandwiches, poor lad. We then stayed over in Kingston and in the evening went to the plush Carib Theatre cinema to see 'Return to the Blue Lagoon', a lot of tosh but we enjoyed the lively comments and vocal enjoyment of the rest of the audience. The unique, huge (nearly 2000 seater) theatre was opened in 1938 as a dual purpose building for live shows and cinema but with the coming of cinemascope the stage was removed. The inspired design creates the illusion of being under the sea.

The next day we all had tea at The British High Commission and the day after we met the High Commissioner's wife, at Devon House to enjoy their superb home-made ice-cream.

Devon House Ice Cream

We then set off for Duckenfield where Mrs White greeted us like long-lost family.

It looks as if Jamaica has taken on board the USA's Halloween madness in a big way, so there are witches and the like everywhere. No signs of Guy Fawkes though!

Lots of Love

Christopher

CHAPTER 22

Five in a Bed

9th November 1991

Dear Mum

Robin has been with us a week and seems to be enjoying himself. We have been to Rocky Point with Brenda and Camille. Both are getting the hang of swimming but once we leave they will not be able to get to the sea to keep up the practice. Robin and Robert are much the same age and they get on well. Last weekend we went to Port Antonio with Robin and he then, with the confidence of youth, bravely set off on the local buses to do some exploring on his own for a few days. He made it past Kingston and stayed with Andrew and Jacquie, the exchange teachers, in Spanish Town. He is very pleased that his total expenses for the trip came to £16.

At last the Jamaican teachers have their pay rise, 38% back-dated to April, which will just about put them back to where they were in March.

❖ ❖ ❖

Sunday 11th November 1991.

Remembrance Day. We shall certainly remember this weekend!

I am sitting on the balcony of Fountain Hotel, Bath. Yesterday we set out to visit Reach Falls on the way to Port Antonio.

We had a violent tropical storm on Friday night and more was forecast but we decided to risk it as Robin was looking forward to the falls which are said to be pretty spectacular although five miles up in the mountains along a narrow winding track. As well as Robin we had Robert and his new friend Annie. She like him is a Peace Corps volunteer and for the next two years is based in a school for unmarried mothers in Port Antonio. School-age baby-mothers are not allowed in normal schools until after they have given birth so this school aims to keep up their education while they are pregnant. She is not having the best of times and is I think rather depressed, not helped by having been robbed twice since she arrived.

Robert has become her rock I think and they make a handsome pair. The five of us set off. It was the first time we have had five in Horatio but the plucky girl took it in her stride. However we had only gone about five miles when the heavens opened again and I had to stop as I could not see through the windscreen. We discussed the advisability of continuing. Annie had been to the falls herself and felt with the rain and the poor gravel track through the hills it was not something we should attempt so we did a bit of a detour and headed instead for Bath.

The weather cleared and we arrived safely at out destination. In slavery days it was the place to be seen for the slave owners and families. As it is up in the Blue Mountains, where it was cooler, they built, or rather had their slaves build, very smart wooden villas there. Many remain but are now much in need of repair.

There is a botanical garden but like so much else in this end of Jamaica it has been neglected. It is supposed to house the oldest breadfruit tree in Jamaica, brought here by Captain Bligh (he of 'The Bounty') as a source of cheap food for the slaves; we have sampled it and it is quite pleasant to eat.

Horatio bravely climbed the three miles steep slope from the village to the Fountain Hotel car-park. Hurricane Gilbert had damaged much of the hotel and it has only just opened after major repairs.

Bob & Annie at Devon House, Kingston

We were made welcome, ordered lunch, then went to immerse ourselves in the baths. At 2:30, rejuvenated by the spa water or possibly by having downed a good lunch, we thought it was time we set off back.

The weather had other ideas. Suddenly the skies darkened, the lightning and thunder started and the gods pulled out their bath plugs, well more tipped the baths upside down. We decided to wait until the downpour stopped as it usually did quite soon after it had started, but not this time. It just kept on coming. The gentle mountain stream of our arrival became a raging, brown, muddy torrent. Waterfalls appeared on the side of the valley opposite the hotel balcony, about 30 feet away, then whole chunks of earth started sliding into the river. Trees floated swiftly by and the noise crescendoed into a roar, the rain so heavy we could hardly see through it. It dawned on us that our chances of getting back to Golden Grove were decreasing by the minute. Three hours went by with no let up. Night fell and still it poured.

We decided that if we had to be high-jacked and taken hostage by the forces of nature, stranded in a hotel was about as good as it gets. I went to reception to phone Mrs White to tell her of our plight but I guess I should not have been surprised to find the telephone line was down. Also trapped with us was a policeman. He had a gun (but of course) and a truncheon and a notebook, but no radio. However he wrote our details in his notebook and promised to phone Mrs White once he got back to his base in Golden Grove, though it seemed to me that the prospects of him reaching his destination were no better than ours.

Bath Landslide

We had some sandwiches at about 8 p.m. and asked if we could book some rooms for the night. Somewhat to our discomfort the hotel only had one room available but we decided that would have to do. The room was small. They had squashed into it a pair of double beds, although the limited dimensions had forced them to combine the two into one continuous entity. We got hold of some quilts and mats and so made a bed on the floor at the end of the double ones for Robin whilst Robert, Annie, Gemma and I climbed into the double beds together. I have no idea whether Robert and Annie had shared a bed before, but I suspect not. However they were well chaperoned!

Of course we had no night-clothes or washing stuff, but Gemma and I stripped to our underwear (we had experienced Hedonism so were not exactly shy, if we ever were) whilst Robert and Annie stayed in their daywear. Four in a bed and the little one said....

In spite of our rather unconventional sleeping arrangements I think we all had a good night and the day dawned overcast but dry. My main worry was that Horatio would not start after her drowning but she looked contented enough in the car-park. We had an excellent Jamaican breakfast of ackee and salt-fish, breadfruit, and dumplings, and then Robin went off to survey the scene. He was soon back. The road was blocked by a large landslide of rocks, mud and a couple of trees about 100 yards down the road. I went down with him to have a look and truly no way would we get Horatio away from the hotel until the blockage was cleared, and this was Jamaica. How long would it take? As they say round here 'Soon come!' which means any time in the next five years.

As we were surveying the scene a local man came clambering over the mire and rocks. His trousers were thick with mud up to his thighs. He cheerfully added to our concern by informing us that there were two more blockages down the road, one even bigger than the one we were surveying. It began to look as if we would be spending a few more nights in our hotel room. I was very worried that Cislyn would be in a blind panic at our failure to return but the telephone was still dead so Robin, Robert & Annie decided to try to get down to Bath and see if they could find a house that still had a working phone. They set off and I sat down and started this letter whilst Gemma and I waited anxiously for their return. We heard on the radio news last evening that a car was swept away near Morant Bay and the road was under four feet of flood water. We were glad that we had decided not to try to leave when the storm broke yesterday.

We discovered that the government owned hotel is 'cash

only' and of course we never travel with our wallets full of Jamaican readies. However after more than a little discussion and pleading they somewhat   reluctantly agreed that they would accept a cheque.

At noon the brave explorers returned, covered in mud. They had managed to escape trying to squelch through the deepest part as a Rastafarian living beside it was charging fifty cents to avoid it by clambering through his garden. I have to admire his initiative. Our friends had reached Bath and phoned Robert's landlady to tell her of our plight. Mrs White was not in. It is Sunday so she would have been at church, no doubt praying for our souls. There seemed to be traffic about, including a bus being towed by a tractor. It had come to a halt in the flood the previous evening on the way from Golden Grove.

Later that day.

We discussed our best plan of action and it seemed we had to abandon Horatio (don't tell David) and make our way to the main road, then try to secure a lift, hoping the road to Golden Grove was not still flooded. Gemma is not good at roughing it but had no choice. A young bare-footed Jamaican offered to help her, which he did, receiving J$20 for his kindness which, whilst not much to me, was probably a small fortune to him So muddy but unbowed we all made it back to Bath via the Rasta-man's garden, though the price of the detour had doubled to J$1 by then! As you know inflation is an ever present feature of Jamaican life.

In Bath we stood hopefully by the roadside but for half an hour not a single vehicle came by. We were somewhat entertained as we waited by watching the efforts of a local trying to remove the hubs from his VW Bug. His tool kit seemed to consist of a mole wrench, a pair of pliers and a hammer and chisel.

I just hope he does not find Horatio and regard her as a ready source of spares for his own car.

Eventually an old van appeared and we asked the driver and his companion if they would take us to Duckenfield. He agreed he would do so for J$100, about £6, which seemed a good deal to us, so we clambered in the back, sat on the floor and bumped and rattled our way back home. Whether the road was still flooded we had no way of telling but we made it and here I am to tell the tale. As we got out near Cislyn's bungalow we saw her struggling up the hill on her way back from church (I have told you before about the long services!). Cislyn was both surprised and delighted to see us as we five mud-covered adventurers clambered out of the back of the van. Her fervent prayers for our safe return had been answered.

So here we are, and there is Horatio, and when the twain will meet is the in the lap of whatever Jamaican authority is responsible for clearing mud-slides. Until then we are stuck and are now wondering how on earth we shall get Robin to the airport for his flight home on Wednesday. To think that on the way out yesterday morning I posted you a letter which said things seemed to have settled down somewhat and life was no longer quite so exciting. Nearly famous last words!

Tonight the Jamaican TV is broadcasting Part Two of 'The Monocled Mutineer', some of which was filmed in the market place, Somerton. Home!!

Lots of love

Your Christopher

CHAPTER 23

Port Royal Buccaneers

15th November

Dear Mum

Back to just two, but what an end Robin had to his stay with us. Much to my amazement, 'Oh ye of little faith', the hotel at Bath Spa phoned late on Monday to say the road had been cleared. I managed to sort out the necessary buses to get me there the following day, much relieved that I would be able to take Robin to Kingston Airport on Wednesday for his evening flight. But yet again the Jamaican weather god had other ideas.

On Monday evening there was another thunderstorm which went on most of the night. In the morning the hotel phone was again not working but I phoned the police station at Bath and was not too surprised to be told that the hotel road was again blocked by more landslides. If Horatio was still stranded Robin and I had planned to catch the bus into Kingston after school on Tuesday and stay at the hostel but we found out that the route to Kingston was still in a bad way with landslips, flooding and the loss of what little tarmac it had so we decided I would take a day off school and we would go in on Wednesday morning, although if we failed to make it I would have to re-book Robin at a cost of £500. I did wonder if hiring a helicopter to Kingston would be cheaper.

Robin spent his Tuesday exploring the area and took some photos from the remains of Duckenfield Great House which had once been the home of the local slave owner. He also photo-graphed the impressive landslip further up our road where the whole bank, coconut trees and all, had slid sideways onto the road, the trees remaining upright and looking as if they had been there forever.

Tuesday evening came and again the heavens opened. I spent much of the night cursing myself for not already being with Robin in Kingston. We rose early and got ready in case the bus made it through and at around 7:30 it arrived. The owner-driver, rejoicing in the name of Sidney Shakespeare (all the slaves had to take their owners' surnames) was Cislyn's friend and had kindly offered to let me stay in Kingston with his family, then return with him on the early (very) bus the following day. So we set off and although the roads had a lot of flood water on them his bus, Aries (perhaps given his surname it should have been Ariel), sailed (almost literally) through the lakes and we arrived safely at the turn to the airport. Sidney told me how to get to his home in Kingston and Robin and I caught a local bus to the terminal. Knowing we had the whole day to fill we thought we would check in Robin's suitcases (he did not travel light like Gemma and I do) and then explore.

Yet another bright idea gone wrong! Although the departure area was empty the lady guard refused to let us enter until 5 p.m. I politely enquired as to where we could leave the suitcases. "We don't have the room for cases." was the terse reply as we were facing an empty area the size of a tennis court. "Try Air Jamaica." We tracked this down but were again informed that there was no room and no one ever left their luggage at the airport. By now more than a little annoyed we headed for the restaurant where we could spend the rest of the day drinking Red Stripe and blotting out the hours in a haze of alcohol. At the restaurant door we were met by a young waiter. "Good morning gentlemen. May I show you to a table? Would you like a drink? Lunch will be served from noon." What manners. We explained our real need was to leave our suitcases somewhere secure. "No problem, sir. I will lock them into our food store." This was accomplished and after leaving what I hoped was a large enough tip we set off on foot to Port Royal.

On the map it did not seem to be that far along the airport causeway which stretches through the scrub and mangroves across Kingston Harbour but it turned out to be about six miles and after three I wondered if we should not give up on the idea. However a pick-up truck stopped and offered us a lift, so we clambered onto the back and travelled Jamaican style sitting on the sides and hanging on tight.

Port Royal was known in the sixteen hundreds as 'the wickedest, richest city on earth'. For 35 years it was the home of the buccaneers of the Spanish Main (from the settlements on the Mainland of Central America) led by Henry Morgan. Spanish ships and the whole Spanish coastal area were continually harassed and robbed by the buccaneers with the tacit approval of the British. Morgan became extremely rich, bought three sugar plantations, was knighted by Charles the Second and became Governor General of Jamaica (which the British had taken from the Spanish in 1655) where he died in 1688.

Pick-up transport

However in 1692 an earthquake sent ninety-percent of Port Royal into the harbour where it remains, like a Caribbean Pompeii under the sea. Port Royal certainly wasn't rich now and didn't appear to be very wicked   either, but it did have a splendid restaurant where we had a lunch of fresh baked fish and bammies (fried cassava cake) for less than £3.

Fort Charles itself was rebuilt after the earthquake and now houses a small but very interesting museum. They are also restoring the cast-iron Victorian hospital, due to open next January though that seemed rather optimistic to me. Not to be missed is 'The Giddy House'. Built to be an ammunition store, it is a testment to the Victorian bricklayers but not to their foundation laying skills as, soon after it was built, one corner dropped several feet leaving the whole building at a crazy angle like a drunk hanging onto a lamp post. Entering it one is completely disorientated and it is well named.

Giddy House, Port Royal

Robin and I decided the whole area was a tourist goldmine but no locals seemed to have thought this and transport to there is almost non-existent. There is a ferry, but it starts out from Lower Kingston, off bounds to any but the most foolhardy tourist.

Pleased with our expedition Robin and I set off back for

the airport terminal. We managed to flag down a tanker to give us a lift and the rest of the day went very smoothly, though that is not a description of us bouncing along in the tanker. Robin checked in and I caught the bus back to Sidney's home where I had a very pleasant evening playing piano duets with the driver's daughter and helping his son with his maths homework. The next morning we would set off at 4:30 so I turned in early and apart from being woken by a huge crash (I think Sidney was cleaning his rather muddy bus and dropped his galvanised bucket) I slept well until 4 a.m.

Sidney's bus is not so very large, 24 seating and 50 standing or as many more that can be squeezed in. Sidney's conductor had overslept and so as we picked up passengers on the way into Kingston it was fairly obvious that many were getting a free ride. In Lower Kingston fire engines were chasing each other around madly. There was a bad fire in some shops and the street hydrants were dry so the firemen had to keep going back to the harbour to collect water. Perhaps not so surprisingly we learnt later from The Gleaner that all of the properties involved had been detroyed. This is all too common in this narrow-laned ghetto where gang warfare rages daily.

The conductor arrived at the bus-station and we set off for Duckenfield at 5:30. It was a beautiful dawn; the sky lightening, glowing pink and gold, followed by the sun, a red ball reflected in the still water of the deep blue Caribbean Sea. The Blue Mountains, so well named, rising majestically on our left. For the second time I thought what a lovely ride that would have made for the tourists but they were still safely imprisoned in their hotels. We picked up quite a few of my pupils and I realised what an early start so many of them had. No wonder they often fall asleep during the day. Quite a few pupils had used the floods of the past week to take an unofficial holiday, so some of my classes were down to single figures. I liked that!

On Thursday morning the hotel phoned. The road was once again open, so after Thursday school I caught a very packed minibus to Bath to rescue Horatio. There were twenty-four of us in the twelve-seater and at one point I was squashed between two large bottoms with a schoolgirl sitting on my lap. Horatio come back, all is forgiven. I guess that the other passenger find it just as distasteful as I do but they have no choice.

Leaving the bus in Bath I set off up the three-mile climb to where I hoped Horatio would be waiting for me. Several people spoke to me on the way and asked if I was going to the hotel to get my car. Obviously our adventure had not gone unnoticed by the locals and I wondered how much of Horatio would still be there, but there she was exactly as I had left her and bless her she started as soon as I turned the key.

I wrote a letter of thanks to The Gleaner to thank the kind waiter who had looked after Robin's cases at the airport. This was printed a few days later and I hope seen by him. My second Jamaican publication.

Love,

Christopher

CHAPTER 24

Taking a Machete to a Banana

Various dates 9.12.91 to 4.1.92

Dear Mum

We are safely back from our fortnight Christmas Holiday in Destin, Florida, which was a lovely change. I hired a car and we drove around the area though there was not a lot to see; many acres of pine trees and a white-sand beach. I was more than a little confused by the instruction on the back of every municipal truck which warned 'Do not follow this vehicle.' Once one was behind it and both of us were going in the same direction on a narrow road it proved an instruction that seemed impossible to obey without pulling over and waiting while it disappeared over the horizon, eventually reaching the destination to which I was not allowed to follow it to. I am pretty law abiding when it comes to driving but this was one rule of the road I felt forced to disobey.

We visited 'Seaside' which impressed us. It is a recently built master-planned community designed by many architects on the so-called principles of 'New Urbanism' with attractive wooden houses. After the laid-back slow pace of Jamaica we found the USA high-pressured. In restaurants if one does not eat ones meal fast enough it is likely to be whipped away unfinished to be replaced by the next course. Perhaps I am becoming too Jamaican?

David has sent us a very expensive Christmas card, a snow scene (try explaining snow to a five-year old Jamaican). When opened it plays 'Silent Night' (we don't get many of those here, what with the insects and the Reggae) and lights come on and off in the church and the houses. Brenda, who now spends a lot of time with us, is entranced by it and we have promised to give it to her. I found it quite hard to buy Christmas Cards in Golden Grove but found instead a set of cards with a man leading a donkey, so I wrote under the picture, 'Mary fell off at the last pothole', which Gemma at least thought was quite funny.

Whilst I seem to be on a biblical theme, when in Destin we visited the Eden Garden State Park and when we were showing Brenda some postcards of Florida she spotted one of the park entrance with the name plate just stating 'Eden'. She obviously knows her Old Testament as this impressed her enormously. I did not want to disillusion her.

"Gosh! Have you been to Eden?"

"Yes."

"Did you go in?"

"Yes"

"Did you see the animals, and the trees, and the fruits?"

"Yes, Yes, Yes. But Adam and Eve weren't there. I think they had been sent out."

"Were the animals all sitting down together? Were they tame?"

"Well, I didn't see any eating each other."

"Gosh! Did you see the apple tree?"

"Yes"

"Wow!"

Mouth wide open for several minutes. I thought the next question would either be "Did you eat an apple?" or possibly "Did you see the snake?", but she was too amazed to question me any further. Was I glad that I had bought the postcard of the entrance sign! On reflection it is probably best that we did not eat any apples in Hedonism.

Last Sunday's Baptist Service was a full megaton up on the previous ones, exciting though they had been. The Youth Club took it under the guidance of Jennifer, one of the teachers from school. In school she is one of the quietest there, though quiet is a relevant term, but once she started her preaching she was suddenly full of sound and fury, the large congregation encouraging her with many cries of "Yes! Yes! Yes, Lord!", "Truly Sister", "Praise be!" and so on, joining in with any quotations from the Bible that Jennifer started. After this had built up to fever pitch the pastor called on those who "Felt the Lord in them." to come to the front. Three ladies, one gentleman and a girl responded. The pastor said a prayer, again highly charged, triggering a hysterical outburst from one of the ladies who threw her arms in the air whilst repeatedly shrieking "Lord Jesus, have mercy." until eventually she collapsed to the floor weeping uncontrollably. Cislyn was much moved by this and told Gemma, who had not come, that she had missed "a lovely service". I am nearly reduced to tears myself when I think how poor they are and how little they have for which to thank the Lord.

Cislyn seems to go to a lot of funerals, always in her Sunday best, and when she returns always tells us "It was a lovely funeral."

Our fellow lodger, the banana plantation guard, has a new female companion. He is already an example of the baby-mother/baby-father syndrome, having two children in Kingston looked after by their baby-mothers. Now with a steady girl-friend here I guess he could soon be fathering another.

Talking of bananas, a little botany lesson for you. The banana plant is the largest herbaceous perennial with a sturdy stem which looks like a trunk. Once the plant has fruited the main stem is cut down and a new shoot from the base replaces it. Cislyn's somewhat wild garden has a banana plant which has fruited and a few weeks ago she told me she would have to get someone in to chop it down. "I'll do that for you." I said. She seemed shocked that a schoolteacher would do such menial manual labour but provided me with a large machete and I chopped it down without too much trouble. I think she was duly impressed. Her garden also has a mango tree (though the mangoes are terribly stringy) and a pine-apple, a smallish shrub which has fruited once. We enjoyed eating that, as we do most of the wide variety of tropical fruits on offer at the market.

Royal View Garden Banana

Whilst I was feeling energetic I decided to repair Cis-lyn's back-door which needed the lintel screwed down. I had found a small box of screws and nails which her husband had saved so set to work, putting the box down on the path. When I turned to get a screw out of the box it had vanished. I was sure that I had not moved it but the heat does funny things to one's brain! Then I remembered that Cislyn's guard dog, Rex, likes collecting things and had a store of items under a bush in the back garden. Yes, there was the box, amongst all the other doggy treasures. My turn to be a re-triever and I was able to complete my repair, the box safely up on the window-sill out of doggy reach.

Gemma is counting the days to our return to you, quite literally as she has made a countdown calendar and crosses off each day as it passes. She offered to do some one-on-one English teaching at school but this has not worked out well as the teacher took Gemma's appearance as a sign that she need not bother to turn up at school herself. Gemma's phar-maceutical training did not equip her to cope with thirty plus Jamaican school-kids.

We have a new caretaker who introduced himself to me the first day of the new term. "Hello, Mr Cox. I'm smelly." There's no answer to that I thought, but it turns out he is a Mr Smellie and a very nice helpful chap too with no B.O. problem. No new principal, but there is talk of one starting at half-term, so it looks as if the vice-principal, who had high hopes, has been overlooked which is sad for her as she has tried so hard to improve things.

Horatio continues to give me fresh problems. When we got back from the USA the battery was flat and a push start did not do the trick. I found the petrol in the carburettor had evaporated and with a flat battery the fuel pump would not run so I ended up sucking the petrol along the tube from the tank! Not the pleasantest of tastes but it did the trick and with a push it roared into life. I have found that the rear chas-sis is splitting in two but my usual Morant Bay repairers have welded over the crack which will hopefully keep Horatio in one piece. How could the MOT document (yes we have those here too) state 'None found.' in the section 'Signs of rust or corrosion'. Perhaps the MOT certificate is not all that it seems. Most things can be purchased here, given enough dollars. The welding took one and a half hours and cost me £4.50. I am going to find English garage repairs rather dear aren't I? However, with imported parts being so expensive, my total bill so far is very close to what David paid for the car. I just hope that he appreciates my efforts.

I recently met the brother of Horatio's deceased owner, Mr Grey, and he seemed amazed that I was actually making long journeys in her. He told me that she was acquired as a hobby just for the fun of doing it up but his brother died before he got started. Tell me about it! Anyway, as I have told you, the car's documents and insurance are still in Mr Grey's name which panicked me when we were stopped at a   police check point. Fortunately the police seemed to assume that Mr Grey was my exchange teacher and I did not argue with this conclusion so we were soon (Jamaican soon) sent on our way.

We have been befriended by a couple in Kingston. He was a diplomat at the British High Commission but he has now retired to a lovely house in Upper Kingston. They have taken Bonnie's two remaining kittens and we have stayed with them a couple of times. The last time we visited we joined them at the Annual Melbourne Cricket Club's Presentation Dinner where we met two West Indian cricketers, Courtney Walsh and Rohan Kanhai, which excited me if not Gemma. With the visiting dignitaries we come across at the High Commission we are most certainly meeting folk that I would not have ever chatted to in England.

The cane cutting season is underway, apparently early this year, which at least means the locals will get some pay. The fields became very attractive as the cane ripened with tall pampas grass plumes turning the whole area from green to fawn. The fire when they set the cane ablaze was intense. Now the fields are full of the blackened stems being cut by hand as in the days of slavery. The trailers scatter their loads over the roads once again.

Our fuel here is Calor gas, which we buy from a Chinese store in Morant Bay where they refill your empty cylinders. The last time I went to replenish our supplies the gas tanker was late arriving; it was due at 11 a.m. but did not appear. There was a long line of empty cylinders and a crowd of men waiting patiently. They do a lot of that around here.

I needed to visit the bank, which did not close until 2 p.m. so I decided to wait for the tanker, perching on a concrete post which had once held the supports for a house. Many of the houses here are on concrete stilts which help to stop the termites entering and building their nests in your roof space. As you may remember our villa's defensives were not termite proof and Mrs White has had to pay a lot of dollars to have a huge nest removed from the attic.

I still do not understand much of the patois, but enough to know that much of the conversation while I waited was understandably about the ever weakening Jamaican Dollar and the hyper-inflation. Some of the group had lit a fire and cooked fish, which when done were eaten on the spot, the men spitting out the bones onto the pavement. Another group erected a makeshift table, brought some chairs over from the small café opposite, and started an enthusiastic game of dominoes, this being a popular pastime here.

One of the waiting customers came up to me. "You don't remember me do you?" I had to admit I didn't. "You helped me when I could not find anywhere to live." he explained. At least I think that was what he said; as usual it was all in Patois. "And who do you think I am?" I asked. "Father." was the inevitable reply. That was four 'Father's' in one day. I have given up correcting people. I just say "Hello. How you doing?" and pass on by. At least it makes me feel better about my continuing difficulty separating one pupil from another at school.

By 1 p.m. I thought that I had had waited long enough so headed into the bank. All I needed to do was pay in some

UK cheques and draw some cash on my Visa card, but such is the form filling, checking, re-checking and more form filling that one needs the patience of Job. The advent of computers has made this complex process even more painful as they still use their many forms as they have done for centuries but all their records have to be entered onto their computers as well. However an hour later I was through, just in time to see their shutters come down.

Still no gas tanker though, so my next port of call would be the tax office to renew the car tax. Apart from being queue jumped twice this seemed to be going OK. Of course the car is still on paper anyway 'owned' by the deceased Mr Grey, but the clerk just assumed that I was he, and it seemed best, not for the first time, to go along with this misconception.

I paid up my J$124 for six months' tax and the clerk filled in the registration certificate. Then I was sent off to another clerk to pick up the tax disk. I guess it was too much to hope that one clerk could fulfil both requirements. The lady then started checking through a ist of prices, which depended on the engine capacity, the number of seats, the use of vehicle and so on. She called over to the first clerk "You've got the man's charge wrong. It should be 162 dollars." then back to me "Give me another forty dollars. You understand?" I understood, I thought, and paid up. Now it would be OK. Oh no it wasn't. Another verbal assault on the first clerk, "You've marked it to May. It should be November." "No." he responded, "He asked for six months tax." "Then it's not 162 dollars." she parried. Then to me, "I'm giving you a years' tax. You gave him 124 dollars which was too much for six months but too little for a year. You got a year's tax now. You understand?" Well I didn't really understand why I could not be given back the excess payment, whatever it was, and have the six months' tax I had originally asked for, but she had already scratched out the 124 and written 162, and changed May to November. There was also probably a strict regulation that you could not be given money back once it had been handed over, so I acquiesced and David now has his car taxed for a whole year at the grand cost of £6 sterling. I just hope Horatio lasts that long.

The good news is that by the time I had done all this the gas store was still open, the crowd had gone, and I was able to refill my cylinders.

And so another day passed.

Quick, Gemma, cross it off on your calendar.

Love

Christopher

CHAPTER 25

Riots, Rustling and Robberies

28th January 1992

Dear Mum

I have been to Kingston to meet up with the other exchange teachers who are here until August. One couple have a problem. She is the teacher but he has no work. They are not married and as a result the immigration authorities have told them he cannot stay in Jamaica for more than six months so will have to go back to the UK in February. We were aware of this rule before we came here which prompted Gemma and I to move our wedding forward otherwise we would have been in the same situation. As most mothers here are not married it does seem rather harsh but I am not sure much can be done about it although they are appealing to The Ministry of Justice to try to get the ruling cancelled.

While in Kingston we visited Stanley, the retired headmaster, and his wife, Fay. He could not cope with being at home all day so although approaching his seventies he is now working full time at a High School in Upper Kingston. Fay wanted a tea-pot which is not easy to find here.

I mentioned this to Kate at the High Commission as she is shortly off to the UK again for another break and she has promised to bring Fay a tea-pot from the UK. Fay is very impressed that she will have a true English teapot arriving in the diplomatic bags! We have promised that once we return to England we will make sure she receives regular supplies of loose leaf tea, which is also quite hard to find in Kingston.

Stanley & Fay

Dear Bonnie is again expecting and after much discussion we have decided to take her to Kingston to live with the retired diplomat and his wife. I think I told you that they took in two of Bonnie's previous brood, but tragically a feral street dog killed them. Better luck this time we hope. We thought it best for Bonnie's new family to have a stable home rather than be abandoned when we leave. Gemma and I will miss her terribly though.

Robert's friend Annie seems to attract thieves. You may recall me telling you that she was robbed twice at the hostel, so she has now moved to a small chalet in Bonnie View Hotel grounds. On her first afternoon there she came back from her duty at the pregnant schoolgirls Centre to find that she had been robbed yet again, losing her cheque book, her credit card, her phone card, J$150 (£4.50) and a bag of things she used at the Centre. Much distressed she reported this to the hotel who promised to put a guard outside her door. Some chance of that!

However she was woken at 4 a.m. the following morning by a tapping on her window. It was the thief, who told her he was ashamed of stealing her things as he did not know she was a volunteer at the Baby-mother Centre. He had brought back her bag and had put it down by the pool. Amazingly to me, Annie then engaged him in a long conversation during the course of which she managed to persuade him to return nearly every-thing else, including the money but not the phone card, which ended up being all that she lost. At first light she went to the pool and recovered her bag. What a courageous girl. Of course there was no sign of a guard.

I am still adding replacement parts to Horatio, the oil pressure switch this week. She is getting a little more reliable and I felt confident enough to take Gemma, Brenda and Camille to the old port area of Bowdens. The bananas used to be shipped out from there but now they all go via Port Antonio. Some en-terprising locals have set up an oyster farm, using bits of car tyres fixed to wooden poles, which appears to be a great success. Nice to see a bit of initiative.

It was a lovely view from the hillside over the water looking towards England. We then took the back road to Rocky Point to give the girls another swimming lesson. Not the best of ideas as the road became a track, eventually ending up across a cane field before we rejoined the 'proper' road by the man-groves. Horatio took it all at a very sedate pace and survived with no harm done. Gemma loves the Mimosa trees by the road-side. They have a beautiful scent though my favourite wild plant is the mauve Jacaranda.

The gang warfare in Downtown Kingston seems to be escalating, or so The Gleaner reports, with police and army on the streets rather like Northern Ireland. Here though it is not religion but political loyalties that cause the trouble. In Jamaica's ghetto districts politics and crime go hand in hand. Two big 'dons' have been killed in the past fortnight. The dons are gunmen who are supported by rival political parties. One was killed in the street but the second was in jail and died in an unexplained fire in his prison cell where he was being held pending extradition to the USA to face murder and drug charges. No court here would dare convict a don as they are protected by their political leaders. The leader of the opposition party, Edward Seaga, led the funeral procession for the first mentioned don. Fortunately our destinations in Kingston are well away from the most dangerous areas.

Our local Anglican church in Golden Grove held a confirmation service on Friday. The Bishop of Jamaica officiated. We suffered a very long boring sermon and some very slow hymn singing. Not at all like the Baptist Church at Duckenfield. Most of the twenty confirmed were well into their 60's and 70's and they included Mr Spencer, our cow-man, who is 95. The poor man has had his bull stolen. The locals were very upset and set out to find the animal, which they did, but too late. It was hanging up in a Morant Bay slaughter-house. We feel so much for the man and doubt that he will be able to replace his prize possession. Cislyn blames the devil, taking his revenge because of Mr Spencer's Church of Jamaica confirmation. Certainly it was a devilish thing to do and we can but hope the sinning perpetrators are identified and punished.

I have been doing my best to support the very keen girl debaters. I think I told you that they came fourth last year under David's guidance. From his many long letters I can see how well he would be able to develop their skills in getting points across. I just wish that I had his talents in this direction. However, sadly they failed to reach the first round in Kingston as their minibus did not turn up. However, having done so well last year, they were given a 'let' and will be able to debate in Round Two, transport difficulties permitting.

It is too far to drive to Negril for our second taste of Hedonism at half term so we are going to fly from Kingston in a small one-pilot plane. I don't think we are living dangerously.

Lots of love

Christopher

CHAPTER 26

There's a Crocodile Behind You

25th February 1992

Dear Mum

We think often of our return to the UK. Gemma will be relieved and I will be glad to have somewhat better behaved classes, although I am delighted with the change in my exam classes. They are working really hard, much more like my UK ones, so I hope that this year's CXC results will be better than in the past, not that this is difficult. I have asked Robert to take them through to their exams; Although untrained he is proving to be a very good teacher. David writes that he will be glad to get back as 'he needs a rest having had to work so hard for the past year for so little pay'. Perhaps he has forgotten how hard teaching is over here but he may well not be best pleased that I have doubled his teaching load since September. No way would I describe it as a rest.

Cislyn is also thinking about our return or, in her case, our departure. She has grown so used to 'Mr Fixit' being around. Gemma and she are good together and Gemma now does excellent Jamaican meals. However Cislyn is worried that she will get an unreliable lodger. The 'banana' guard has left owing two months' rent, kept his house key and a gas cylinder, and owes J$100 to Cislyn's neighbour and J$60 to the shop. Cislyn says "They are all thieves around here." though it is not clear why she thinks the rest of Jamaica is different but as she grew up in St Elizabeth in the west she may be right.

The school is taking part in the Junior Achievement Project. Perhaps because it is an idea imported from the USA Robert has been put in charge and has decided on founding The St Thomas Banana Chip Production Company. The worthy idea is that pupils set up the business, issue shares, and hopefully make a huge profit. Sadly, and perhaps not too surprisingly, the pupils were none too keen to take part so Robert has done most of the work himself. He set up a clever solar drying unit and experimented with various banana slicing methods and different drying times. Sadly he did not allow for Jamaican insect life and his project has had to be abandoned because his sun-dried chips kept being invaded and ruined by fruit flies. These are of course used for experiments in laboratories because they reproduce so rapidly and boy did they reproduce on his banana chips. I am sad for the lad but relieved that I only bought one share in his company!

Fruit flies are not his only annoyances recently as, for reasons best known to her, his mum sent him a card for Valentine's Day which came in the school post and caused him no little embarrassment, provoking much mirth amongst the staff. Whether he also had a card from Annie is not something he is prepared to reveal.

The acting head, confident that she would be the next Principal, started getting teachers to cover for absent colleagues. When I first came this seemed a novel idea and classes were left to do their own thing. I guess the change is not universally popular, including with yours truly, as I have had some difficult classes to supervise. However a few weeks ago I took an English class. No work had been set so I decided I would play 'Hangman' with them; you know: guessing letters in a word and drawing a gallows in stages for wrong guesses. This seems not to have reached our corner of the world but it has now caught on big time and in many a classroom since I have seen chalked gallows on the blackboards. I must be going to leave my mark on the school if only for my teaching them a rather sick game! It may be not quite the way I want to be remembered.

The debaters made it to Kingston for Round Two last week

armed with speeches written by another teacher and myself. Of course they should have written the speeches themselves but, when they had not done so a couple of days before, we decided we would have to do it for them. The result has not yet been announced but I rather hope they do not get through to Round Three as I have better things to do with my time

I am treating Gemma to a birthday present of a weekend in the very expensive 'Jamaica Palace' hotel on the way to Port Antonio. She is looking forward to that.

My suggestion that the exchange teachers met up in Kingston once a month is working well. We meet on a Friday and then have the weekend in Kingston. To their relief the Ocho Rios teacher partner's appeal against him being deported was allowed. However the one who ended up with a baby last time round has been conspicuous by her absence. The talk is that she has a new 'man'. Two of our (married) exchange friends have a baby on the way. It will be born in Jamaica but the midwives get plenty of practice so I guess all will be well.

After the last meeting we visited Kingston Zoo and Botanical Garden rather wished we hadn't. The gardens were run down with no plants labelled. The zoo had some sad lions, crocodiles and snakes, all in (separate!) concrete boxes. It was awful but we resisted the urge to give them their freedom. The entry charge was J$2, or sixpence UK. No wonder it was in a bad way.

We have a few crocodiles in our St Thomas swamp though most live on the south coasts's Black River. They seem to keep themselves to themselves and it is a lucky tourist who, having paid for a boat trip, actually catches sight of one. However one day a pupil brought a baby one to school in a cardboard box which gave me a bit of a shock. This American crocodile is apparently much less aggressive than their African or Australian relatives but I don't wish to put this to the test.

Love

Christopher

CHAPTER 27

Birthday Suits in Hedonism

4th March 1992

Dear Mum

Here we are at Hedonism again, but this time for five days. It was a much easier journey in our little aircraft than in Horatio. However Negril Airport only takes local planes and has just a tiny strip of tarmac. The terminal building is a little wooden hut and the white Jamaican stationed there is the booking clerk, security official, baggage loader, and flight controller. The pilots must find their journeys much more fun than sitting for hours in the cockpit of a 747 while the plane flies itself.

Of course we flew very low, 2000 feet to Montego Bay, then at 5500 feet to Negril. I know this because I was sitting just behind the pilot! It was fascinating to see the country from the air. I had not realised there were so many small isolated farms. We also saw several expensive villas complete with swimming pools. Not many of those around Duckenfield.

Poor Horatio has been injured, but not fatally. On our last visit to Kingston I allowed my attention to be distracted by a local falling off his bicycle and spilling his sack of rice over the road thereby failing to notice that the car in front had stopped and I hadn't. I did my best to do an emergency stop but in Horatio this is more a case of 'stamp and pray' so we slid gently into a substantial rear bumper. (I had much the same feeling when the plane landed at Negril and I watched the boundary hedge rapidly approaching, but I couldn't reach the plane's brake pedal.) Fortunately Horatio is anything but substantial so there was no damage to the other car but she has a slightly dented front hood which should be easy to sort out. A shame as after all the new parts I have fitted she has at last become very well behaved and I hope that I shall be handing back to David a fully functioning car, so different from how she was last April.

The school has a new Principal, Mr Symes. He had only been there two days when we broke up for half term but he has really made his presence felt. Already the pupils have decided that they do not like him. I told them that this was all to the good. However I fear he will have to tread a little more carefully if he is not to alienate the staff to the point of rebellion. All the things I have been complaining to you about he has charged at head on (forgive the pun). That is not to say change is not needed but maybe better to deal with the minor things later? He told me he was horrified by the noise, by the pupils' lack of respect for their teachers and by the generally slack atmosphere. He has told the staff that school starts as 7:55 a.m. and they are to be there at this time. He threatened late-comers with a pay-cut. Apparently the regulations allow late minutes to be added together and when they reach 6½ hours then a day's pay can be docked. As he put it "Persistent offenders we can do without." Oh dear, do I see trouble ahead?

Well, it is raining in Negril (apparently the first rain of the year) so we are off to sit in the cool water of the Jacuzzi....

Later

I must have been enjoying myself as it is now Saturday 7th March and we have to pack to go 'home'. We love the utterly relaxed friendly atmosphere here and have chatted to lots of interesting people including a doctor from Peru, a teacher from Canada, a German businessman from Ecuador, an Italian shoe designer from Rome, and lots of Yanks. Gemma and I have decided that the United Nations could do worse than meet each other naked in a communal Jacuzzi in the interests of goodwill to all men. We have been invited to holiday at their homes by several couples and could do a world tour visiting them all.

We would love to come back in the future but it will be a very expensive to do so from England. Many folk do keep coming back though. One lady has been twenty-seven times and a lot are into double figures.

Gemma cried at the thought of going back to Duckenfield but it is only for a few weeks now. Her Jamaica Palace birthday treat had to be put off as dear Horatio was in for his hood repair but we have re-booked for a fortnight's time so she has that to look forward to.

◆ ◆ ◆

Sunday 8th March

Safely back. Hedonism laid on a free car to take us to the airstrip where we caught the De Havilland Twin Otter. There was only one other passenger besides us so we felt we had our own private plane. However we had to change planes at Montego Bay. We waited all day for the flight back to Kingston and that was running an hour late. As we started down the runway we suddenly veered off onto the grass and went back to the terminal. Trouble, I thought, but no; two passengers had just turned up so we had gone back for them.

At Kingston I had the usual haggle with a taxi-driver trying to treat us as gullible tourists. The driver did comment that we could not blame him for trying it on which I guess is fair enough when they earn so little and inflation is so awful. He drove us through all the worst parts of Lower Kingston but it seemed quiet thank goodness. The Gleaner reports that today is the funeral of the 'don' who died in his cell. This time the procession will be led by Michael Manley, the prime minister.

We spend the night at the Indies Hotel, where we had left Horatio. We slept well after much enjoying a splendid Indian meal at The Kohinoor, all for £12. Can't be bad.

A beautiful sunset tonight. Negril is famed for its sunsets but we have not seen a single one while we have been there. However we have had some splendid ones in Duckenfield although they do not last long this far south as we are spinning at nearly 1000 mph rather than the 580 mph of England. Maths lesson over for today!

Jamaican Sunset

The drive back from Kingston was lovely, the sea all shades of blue and the mountains looking splendid. We stopped to buy some naseberries from a roadside stall and waved at our church friend Nell at her 'First and Last Inn' in Stokes Hall. We love the fruit here. The naseberries are plum shape and size with a deep brown medlar colour and a very sweet fudgy taste. We also adore the delicate taste of the Otaheiti apples which are pear shaped with white flesh and a large stone, like an avocado, which we replace with a little ice-cream. What luxury!

Cislyn and the girls have missed us I think. While we have been away the banana packers long strike has finished, but the sugar workers have been out all week. The unions are demanding a 200% pay rise whilst the company have offered 55%. The workers will have no pay this week and the sugar is spoiling in the field. The small independent sugar farmers are in danger of going bankrupt because with nowhere to send their sugar they have to leave their fields uncut and the canes will rot if the strike goes on too long.

Let's hope the teachers do not follow suit and walk out if Mr Symes goes too much over the top. They have become so used to their slack ways that it will be hard to turn things around. The last few weeks could be even more interesting.

Love

Christopher

CHAPTER 28

A New Broom Trying to Sweep Clean

11th March 1992

Dear Jen

It was lovely to receive your letter with all the news of David and the school. I have forgotten what a word-processor is but it seems to do nice neat printing!

Our new Principal continues to threaten the future of life as we know it. Much reform is certainly needed here but the pace could be less frenetic. The promise of a pay cut, or even a sacking, did get 90% of the staff here on time this morning. The future of the other 10% is as yet unclear.

The pupils may not be so easy to get into line. He suspended a pupil yesterday for some misdeed but the lad refused to leave the premises. The next thing we heard was a police car drawing up with two policemen, guns at the ready as always. They had been summoned to evict the obstreperous pupil.

Today Mr Symes has announced a 'Keep Right' rule when moving between rooms. Up to now movement has been Jamaican style push and shove. Will the new rule catch on? Somehow I doubt it.

There are such contrasts here. This morning a group of girls sang 'The School Song' which has been written by the Baptist preacher. They sung with such feeling and panache it was hard not to well up.

I wonder how the pupils are feeling about my imminent departure. I have grown fond of them in spite of the many problems and I hope that they will miss me as I shall miss them.

Mind you Mr Symes is now trying to persuade me to enrol on the staff. No way!! There are some good things here including the wonderful scenery once you leave the squalor behind, fantastic sunsets, delicious food, friendly people, some great swimming, not to mention us lording it in the British High Commission. Careful, I shall talk myself into staying after all! What a year it has been and I have no regrets about my decision to come. It is a pity that David does not feel the same way about his year with you. In his last letter he tells me he is not going to keep teaching but is 'going into shipping', whatever that means.

Enjoy your last few weeks of power!

Best wishes.

Chris

◆ ◆ ◆

15th March 1992

Dear Mum

Only four weeks to go. The new Principal seems certain to make it an interesting month. He continues to fire broadsides but given how little effect it seems to be having I am reminded of Shakespeare's 'Full of sound and fury, signifying nothing.' I do wonder how much experience of the classroom he has; he came here from being a lecturer at the university. I can't think why he has changed jobs but I have a feeling he will regret the move.

Following her intimate behaviour with the car in front in Kingston Horatio has been at the repairers all week and on Friday I was told she was ready so I caught the minibus to Morant Bay (only 26 on board the 12 seater this time) to pick her up. When I got there they were still fixing some of the bits back on but they have made a pleasingly great job of repairing the damage and their respray of the front half is excellent. After two hours sitting on an old car seat while they finished their task they pronounced it ready to drive home. I got in but it was getting dark and I then found that they had not connected up the lights. That was soon sorted.

Whilst observing them re-fixing things (all in the open – they have no building) I thought the mechanic was having difficulty screwing the rusty chrome headlight cover back on but eventually he seemed to have succeeded The bill was J$2200, about £65 today (and even less tomorrow) which is undoubtedly a small or maybe large fortune to a Jamaican earning J$31 a day for cane cutting but seemed very reasonable to me. I paid up and set off back here.

On the way, in the dark, I drove over a discarded drinks can which clattered a bit. I should have realised that this was an unlikely event as out here drinks either come in bottles or boxes (we have box-milk, box-juice and so on). But as I put Horatio to bed for the night I noticed, as you have probably guessed, that she was missing one rusty chrome headlight surround.

I retraced my route at dawn but could not find the missing part. I will have to visit the second-hand spares shop in Kingston. Honestly, if it ain't one thing it's another. I am cross with the mechanic as he must have known the surround was not fixed in properly. Let's hope it is the only thing not replaced properly, although being rear-engined and air cooled there isn't much of a critical nature at the front, under the 'hood'.

Writing of box drinks reminds me to get in some boxes of egg-nog from Miss Maisie at the local shop. This is a drink popular in the States and usually served at Christmas, but here I can get it in a box all year round. The version I buy is innocent enough, if rather overloaded with carbohydrates. It contains 'heavy' cream, milk (straight, evaporated and condensed) and brown sugar besides assorted spices and of course egg yolks. The proper Jamaican version adds in lashings of white rum and bourbon!

Lower Kingston seems unusually quiet at the moment although The Gleaner reports that there have been quite a few holiday cancellations by nervous Americans. Prime Minister Michael Manley is retiring. His replacement seems likely to be his finance minister, P. J. Patterson.

Right, I'll toddle round the corner and get some boxes of (non-alcoholic) egg-nog.

See you soon

Love

Christopher

CHAPTER 29

Two Nights in a Palace

Jamaica Palace

22nd March 1992
Dear Mum

Gemma has had her delayed birthday treat in The Jamaican Palace Hotel which we have passed many times on our trips to Port Antonio. We first took Bob up to visit Annie and we had our last Jamaican meal as a foursome.. In Port Antonio I spotted a 'Bug' looking in worse condition than Horatio was when we first had her. She also was missing one headlight surround but had the one that I ran over. I hoped the owner would sell me his one but he wouldn't as he said he was going "to do it up." I don't envy him.

Annie still seems to attract the criminal element as Robert put his bag down under his chair while we were eating and at the end of the meal it was missing. He found it in the loo, minus his (inexpensive) camera, which he was taking for repair as it had gone wrong, two Swiss army knives, and a set of biros. Nothing too serious but upsetting.

We said our farewell to Annie but hope to meet up in the States some time and we drove back to our hotel. It does look like a palace with its marble columns and black and white theme marble floors. It was built not so very long ago by a German countess who must have poured many many millions of Marks into it. She was there to greet us as we drove up to the impressive entrance portico. Sadly her dream palace has turned into a nightmare. She has made at least two bad errors of judgement. It is in the wrong place, as few holidaymakers come to this poor eastern end of Jamaica, and it is inland with no beach, which most visitors would expect to be part of their Caribbean hotel experience. So next week it comes up for auction.

The first evening we were the only guests and indeed felt like a king and queen, the many waiters and staff competing to impress us with their deferential service. Two other guests arrived on the Saturday but I would think it was built to cater for several hundred. Although very expensive compared to the other local hotels the facilities did not justify this. For instance we had a beautiful chandelier in the bedroom with a moulded plaster ceiling complete with cornice and rose (though no mirror!) but we were lacking a phone or hot water.

Our meal in honour of Gemma's birthday was a veritable feast. Fish mousse on potato pancakes, heart of palm salad, and a very tender succulent steak with croquette potatoes, finishing with a mouth-watering lemon sorbet. The chef did us proud. We told him how much we had enjoyed his culinary skills. Sadly I fear he will shortly be looking for alternative employment.

On Saturday we lounged by the large pool which was a marble map of Jamaica with the major coastal towns labelled. I managed a swim from Port Antonio to Negril, 180 miles though not quite so far when scaled down. Gemma does not like being out of her depth so only managed Kingston to Ocho Rios For real this would mean swimming across the Blue Mountains which would be quite a swimming triumph. My swim, although possible to do it do it for real, would involve covering nearly three-quarters of the Jamaican coastline if you swam clockwise.

Gemma enjoyed being 'Lady Muck' and when we left we took a photo of her at the front portico being shown to her carriage (aka Horatio) by a liveried footman.

The Jamaican dollar is still heading downhill at frightening speed with the inevitable rise in prices of imported food and goods. This week we hit J$40 to the £1. It was J$15 when we arrived. Workers' wages have nowhere near kept up so the poverty just worsens by the week. What a contrast between the Jamaica Palace hotel and the dirt of Duckenfield.

Your Carriage Has Arrived

A sad end to this letter. Sorry.

Your Christopher

CHAPTER 30

Gold Teats

29th March 1992

Dear Mum

Happy Mother's Day.

We have made our last planned drive to Kingston. Horatio behaved perfectly and the spare-parts store found a headlight rim for her, all shiny so it rather shows up the other one. They would not take any payment. That is a first for Jamaica. Gemma enjoyed the shops (again) and bought a pair of Jamaican lobe-lengthening earrings for her pierced ears; no comment. We visited Bonnie and her new brood of kittens. They are lovely, but clearly Bonnie is being wildly spoilt as she has become rather portly.

David tells me he is going to register Horatio in his mother's name. She is a headmistress and the idea is that the Ministry of Education will pick up the car bills. Just credible I guess. I gather that he has had a small accident with my Metro but is getting it repaired. That makes me feel less guilty about my failed emergency stop a few weeks ago.

Talking of accidents, I nearly burnt down Mrs White's house one morning last week. I was, as usual, burning up the rubbish in her garden using a bit of old roofing 'zinc' to surround the flames but somehow a dead branch on the mango tree caught alight. A couple of buckets of water put that out, or so I thought, and I set off for school. Fortunately Gemma looked out shortly after I had left and saw that the branch had re-ignited. The 'house-girl' who washes our sheets and cleans for Mrs White ('girl' is a bit of an exaggeration as she must be in her eighties) was there and put the fire out, permanently this time, using a hose-pipe.

Mr Symes continues to berate the staff and pupils for all their many sins. His threat on Friday was to send back home every pupil who is not in school at 8 a.m. I agree late arrivals are a problem, but now I have seen the difficulty getting transport I understand the reasons. I don't know if he thought the evicted pupils would go home, rather than frequent a local bar, but I guess the threat will not be carried out any more than the dsnger of losing pay will stop some staff turning up late. By last Friday we had 31 staff on site for the start of school and 14 arriving as the morning wore on. Maybe the usual transport difficulties maybe? Or was it last night's ganja?

Last Tuesday Mr Symes had a parents and pupils meeting for Grades 7 to 9, the younger pupils. About thirty parents turned up and it was then their turn to be harangued for not getting their children to school on time and in the correct uniform, like blue socks with black shoes. Actually the school uniform is one thing that does not need to improve as it generally is closely adhered to, though the poorest children tend not to have socks of any colour and often their clothes are torn or patched. He also complained to the parents about girls with gold teats. Well I thought that was what he was implying, though I dread to think how he would have known. However the penny dropped; As with the Duckenfield 'taiter' it was the seeming inability of the locals to pronounce 'th' so it was actually gold teeth he was complaining about. Apparently it is all the rage amongst the girls to stick gold foil onto their teats, sorry teeth, using superglue (which is called 'crazy glue' here). Cannot say that I had noticed gold foil stuck to any part of their anatomy but that is probably my poor observational skills.

On Wednesday a boy read a prepared apology in morning devotion (school assembly). He was begging to be forgiven and taken back into school. His crime was putting a knife to a teacher's throat and threatening to finish her off if she ever again dared to tell him to stop eating in class. Anyway he has said "Sorry" so that all seems to be OK then. If this is to be the punishment for something so serious I fear for their future.

It is not just pupils who commit grievous crimes. At the final exchange teachers' seminar Andrew and Jacquie who teach in Lower Kingston told us that one of their staff beat up a pupil. The next day the pupil brought in a gang to take revenge and in the ensuing fracas the teacher chopped off the kid's thumb with a machete he had confiscated from another pupil. They did not know what, if any, action would be taken but the teacher was continuing to teach, and presumably to assault, his pupils. We think that they are very brave to be teaching in such a school in such a violent area, especially with Jacquie eight months pregnant. What have I been complaining about?

Mind you, as perfect examples of marital bliss, us exchange teachers are not exactly setting a very good example. Gemma and I are both on second marriages after divorces. Two more pairs are not married. One other teacher is separated and living with her Jamaican baby father, whilst yet another is a baby mother and chaser of Jamaican men, or rather their willing quarry.

We have always enjoyed a good Friday meal at the Ministry of Education but for reasons not disclosed the entire canteen staff 'left' last Monday and the canteen was closed. Now can there be a connection with the Ministry Audit now going on? Apparently no accounts had been done since 1987 and they were uncovering all sorts of fiddles and inexplicable bills and expenses, which included some for people still apparently on the pay roll but no longer working there!

Anyway, instead of a canteen meal, we all went off to the nearby 'pattie' shop. I shall miss the Jamaican patties, a smaller version of Cornish Pasty, but usually with spicy meat. Come to think of it I am going to miss an awful lot of wonderfully scrumptious foods. Perhaps we can find a Jamaican store and perhaps a restaurant in Bristol, where there is a large Caribbean immigrant population.

Although our Duckenfield neck of the woods is less violent than most of the nation we have not been spared. I told you of the murder last year of a pupil and her mother. Yesterday there was a domestic dispute in our village and 17 year old baby mother killed her 29 year old baby father. I also saw that a police car was going into school on Saturday afternoon, but I have not heard what that was about. The Gleaner reports that there have been 140 violent deaths in Jamaica so far this year, the police being responsible for 47 of them, and not surprisingly, given the amount of overtaking on blind corners that we see, about 100 deaths in road accidents; these seem not to count as 'violent'.

With three (or 'tree'!) weeks to go I have been thinking about what I say to folk back home who ask "How was Jamaica?" Unfortunately Charles Dickens got in first: "It was the best of times. It was the worst of times." How true.

Probably we have made our final visit to Rocky Point with the two girls where Camille has swum without her floats for the first time. Sadly, with no transport, I doubt that they will be able to go to the beach again once we have left. The insect life puts off any thoughts of 'a day on the beach' and we can only go on weekend mornings as the sand-flies and mosquitoes are always a dreadful menace in the afternoons. The biting tiny sand flies attack in their millions and it is a case of strip and run into the sea at high speed else we end up blacked-up as if ready for a minstrel show.

See you soon

Christopher

CHAPTER 31

A Jamaican Style Barbecue

1st April 1992

Dear Mum

I have asked Jen to explain to David about All Fools' Day' in England as it is not observed here (as far as I can tell) and the UK kids always try it on with their teachers.

You may remember my cynical report on the ground-cutting ceremony for the new staff flats. It has turned out that my scepticism that they would ever be built was unkind as they have 'completed' the first building over the past few months. Raj and Naomi are the first tenants in the upper storey and they invited us round to see it. Not though because they were proud of their new abode. The stairs to and from the front door are on the outside of the house, eastern style. If one forgets to make a sharp left turn when leaving then there is a plunge of ten feet or so to the concrete path below. Somewhat lethal. We are all shocked at the state of the place. Paint and cement is splashed all over the inside and one of the windows is not fixed into the wall and looked ready to fall out at any moment. It has three rooms plus a small kitchen, but no cupboards or any storage space. The kitchen taps (did you note the plural?; indeed there are two although no hot water system) are purely ornamental as even the cold does not yield any water. The very few electric points are yet to be tested as the electricity company hasn't (yet) connected the property to the mains. Raj, a keen 'do-it-yourself-er' , a superb wood crafter and furniture maker, has run a cable across the scrub from the school canteen. At least he won't have an electricity bill to pay.

The New Flat

To add to their woes Naomi has lost several items of jewellery. She blames the workmen still at work jerry building the downstairs flat. It gets worse. Last week they noticed two of their chickens ' had disappeared' and after investigating it was found that two pupils had taken them, begged to borrow a cooking pot from the school canteen, lit a fire at the back of school, and cooked the chickens. It is no wonder Naomi is as keen as Gemma to leave Jamaica.

Mr Symes chaired a three-hour meeting with both vice-principals and me last week. Jamaican discussions make Hampton Court Maze look like a Roman Road. There was a huge row about the unfairness of sending to cover for another teacher who had not arrived any one found unwisely in the staffroom having a free-period. Then we argued around the reason for every lesson being a different length. Next on the agenda was the text-book problem. If a pupil is either promoted or demoted during the school year and find their new class is using a

146

different textbook they have not been able to change to the new book. Text books are rented by the pupils in September and the school rules do not permit the switch of the borrowed book until the next September. I could not work out quite why this was the case, but the deputy head was adamant that there was no way this rule could be relaxed. A furious row over it developed ranging from how badly the previous headmaster ran the school to quotations from the Bible!

We rounded this off with discussing one of the staff whose nominal role is 'Work Experience Tutor', which involves about twenty pupils at a time being send to work at a local establishment like 'The Sugar' for three weeks at a time. Mr Symes has discovered that she is on a 'Senior Teacher' pay scale but has no timetabled lessons so either does not bother coming to school or whiles away her day gossiping in the staffroom. I guess she will not be best pleased if her rather cushy life-style comes to an abrupt end.

We had a lunch-time staff meeting which is an improvement on the previous system when the classes were just left to their own devices while the staff met. However Mr Symes continues to grumble at the staff about everything. I can see he is justified in doing this but I fear that the more he moans the less the staff will co-operate with him. There is no sense of "Let's get this place sorted out together chaps." My teaching also became even more difficult today as Mr Symes has decided to 'develop' the old school playing-field outside my room. With no window glass I had to shout to make myself heard over a bulldozer which was levelling the field.

"Are you coming back after Easter?" asked 10/1, my favourite class.

"No, I am not."

"Why?"

I could have told them, and how, but just said that I had to go back to my job in England.

Many children, and the school cooks, ask me to take them back to England when I go. Who can blame them? But I come back home to you with no regrets, neither at coming in the first place, nor at having to leave.

Brenda did not go to school today as her mother told me that she could not afford the J$5, about 12½ pence for her lunch and fees; I would gladly have paid this is she had asked me. Jamaica is also in drought. Even the normally wet parish of Portland is dry and locals are having to walk many miles, either to a standpipe or to any river that still has water in it. Even the palaces of Upper Kingston are only allowed eight hours of water a day.

Horatio is behaving herself, although I have a nasty feeling she is saving something up to surprise me in my last few days here. Only a week and David should be back. How will that go I wonder?

Soon Come

Christopher

CHAPTER 32

Another Lovely Funeral

5th April 1992

Dear Mum

It is our penultimate Sunday here. "Thank God!" says Gemma. I went to the Baptist Chapel service with Cislyn this morning. Two and a half hours, so a short one today. It was as usual alternately deeply moving and hysterical. One difference was that everyone was in black as the lad murdered by his baby-mother in Duckenfield had been a member of the chapel Youth Fellowship. The clergy rant about the evils of drink, gambling, dancing, smoking, ganja; they do not seem to dare to tirade about having babies so casually. I guess many of the faithful are baby-mothers themselves. That must certainly include the organist, whose little boy is a right pest. It is one of the big social problems of Jamaica but no one is seriously tackling it as far as I can tell.

Cislyn has been wearing her black two days running as yesterday she went to an Anglican funeral. She did not disappoint me on her return many hours later. "How was it?" I asked. "Oh, it was a lovely funeral." she enthused. "Such a lot of cars and the church full of flowers with wreaths costing J$300 (£7.50 to me). Truly a lovely funeral. Thank God." She has a heart of gold and the faith that moves mountains. When she goes I am sure they will do her proud and I know what her first words will be when she gets to St Peter at the Gates of Heaven!

With so few weddings I guess funerals are the big social gatherings around here. However I saw there were two 'Banns' notices on the church notice board when I walked past so maybe Easter Weddings are in vogue as they are in England.

I told you I had a feeling that Horatio was saving a final surprise for me. I was right; I stopped at the school yesterday morning to take some slides for my planned illustrated talks when I return. When I came to leave I put my foot on the clutch and nothing at all happened. I let her run down the hill in neutral to pick up speed then managed to get her into first gear and coaxed her back to Royal View Villa. I thought the cable might have broken but it was OK. There was just an ominous click from the clutch housing when I pushed the pedal. Somehow I managed to get all the way back, yet again, to the repairers in Morant Bay. If the engine had stopped on the level road it would have meant a tow. Maybe in that case I could flag down a J.P.S. land-rover as payback for Horatio's sterling effort back in May. Not needed as fortunately I made it all the way in third gear.

After delivering Horatio to the A & E department I went to wait under a thorn tree for transport back here. After a quarter of an hour I was able to flag down a minibus. It was rather full (!!) but the two large ladies on the bench seat next to the driver squashed up a bit more and I was able to rest one cheek on the edge of the seat and let the other hang in the opening by the door so I made the twelve miles back. The charge was J$7, or 17 pence.

David returns on Thursday I think; it is a somewhat grey area. I hope the car is repaired by then or I shall be embarrassed. If they have to take the engine out again, plus get hold of spare parts, it could be David will not have his car when I leave. Fortunately a friend is picking him up from the airport.

A fairly uneventful week at school, though that is a relative comment. My remarks of last week about the erratic lengths of lessons led to me being asked to rewrite the timings which I have done and I have again set the automatic clock timer. It is a complex operation so I have written them an instruction sheet headed 'The Bells! The Bells!'

Mr Symes continues to set me up on a pedestal which

is embarrassing and undeserved but I very much admire his efforts to improve things in the school. Boy are they needed, but he, like the previous head, is clearly finding our staff and pupils a tough nut to crack. I try to be on time every morning but Bob tells me that any staff that arrive after 8 a.m. but before 9 a.m. write 8 a.m. as their time of arrival anyway and at 9 a.m. the vice-principal picks up the register and draws a line under the last 8 a.m. arrival so that anyone getting there by 9 a.m. was there at eight! For every rule be sure a Jamaican will find a way to avoid obeying it. I hope that is not a racist comment.

Wednesday 15th is the big 'Hello to David' and 'Farewell to Chris' party at school, then on Friday the previous head is transporting us to Kingston and in 336 hours we should be home with you. I think it will just be two of us, although Brenda's dad ('Pluggy' as he is known, presumably because of his aforementioned plumbing credentials) said he wishes we could take Brenda back to England with us. Surrogate parents are not unusual here so they would see nothing odd in that but Gemma and I are too old to get into child rearing even if we wanted to and we don't, fond of Brenda and Camille though we are. Camille has passed the exam to go to the High School at Port Antonio and I have offered to pay her fees for her five years there. It would be so good if she could get qualified for a good job and get herself out of the poverty trap.

How I shall miss being here and not just because the Tia Maria is cheap enough at our exchange rate to put a slug into our morning coffees!

We have made so many good friends. I walked to school this morning with Mr Spencer and his two cows. Gemma has given him a copy of the photo I took of the four of them before the tragic loss of his bull and he tells me that he has framed it and hung it in his room to remind him of us. Cislyn will I know be at a loss without 'My people' as she calls us but we will write and phone her regularly.

We shall miss The Gleaner and its daily rants. I don't think I have told you this already but at Christmas they missed printing the daily TV guide for two days. The result of this is that every day now the TV guide is for two days before, so that on Friday they will print the programmes for the previous Wednesday. It seems no one has noticed! As there is only one Jamaican channel we just have to watch whatever is on anyway so it does not really matte to us.

Of course Upper Kingston folk have their huge satellite dishes and can watch American TV to their hearts content. From what I saw of it in Destin they are welcome to it. Jamaica TV has royally entertained us with lots of UK programmes, 'Allo Allo', 'To the Manor Born', 'Dads' Army' and so on.

Let's hope I get good news of a mended Horatio in the morning.

Love

Christopher

CHAPTER 33

Foot Down Miss Davis

7th April 1992

Dear Mum

As you already know, Horatio is in Port Morant car hospital. Her engine is yet again separated from her body and they have found that she has a broken lever inside the clutch housing. The chief surgeon hopes to get a spare lever from Kingston today and then will fit it tomorrow. I hope he will as David is due back any day and I dread to think of his reaction if he finds I do not have his car in Duckenfield.

Today I decided to try to teach Mr Symes and the vice-principals the procedure to set the bell-ringer. They found it hard to understand so I don't think they will manage it when I have left. I am being plagued with requests from the pupils to donate my property to them when I go; my watch, my pencil sharpener, my biro, my calculator, my umbrella, etc. I think they would happily send me back to the UK naked. I know they have so very little, many of them genuinely malnourished, and neglected; hungry for food and affection. Talking of food, I have promised to take Brenda and Camille to see if The Gut Buster is open so that I can buy them each an ice-cream.

Naomi and Raj have had more trouble at the newly built school flat. The Jamaican Electricity Company (JEC) came to connect them up to the mains a few days ago. When Raj put on the lights that evening all the fluorescent tubes blew and their fridge became very agitated. They got JEC back and they found out that the electricians had wired the property into the wrong cable, supplying 190 volts instead of the standard 110. Honestly! I despair.

❖ ❖ ❖

9th April

One day nearer to England! I shall miss each day's excitement though. Yesterday school held an extended 'Devotion' which went on for nigh on 1½ hours. It was interesting, or depressing, or hysterical or maybe all tree (Oh dear. I have caught the Jamaican 'th' problem!). It was led by the young male teachers, some of them more competent than others. One started to sing 'The Lord's My Shepherd" ('Val-dere, val-dera', remember?) but he forgot the words half way through. Another sang out of tune to an even more out of tune guitar. Then we had The Lord's Prayer, but they got that wrong too. However the young mathematics teacher gave an excellent talk, so it wasn't all bad.

We next had the formal 'Apologies'. 'Mea Culpa. Mea maxima culpa.' Tree of the girls had been caught in a local bar during school hours. Each apology was greeted with giggles from the rest of the kids. Their punishment, apart from the public apologies, was to be banned from school for tree days, presumably so that they could spend their free time in the bars with a clear conscience.

Mr Symes then addressed the school. He started with a long tirade about incorrect uniform and school badge. He then told us that he had purchased a cane and was going to use it until the pupils learnt to behave and he would be using it "on your most fleshy part." This brought the house down! He then threatened to line up the whole 9th grade boys and cane them one after the other in front of the whole school, presumable the innocent along with the guilty. Maybe this did not sound as unlikely to the pupils as it did to me as that seemed to shut them up and we were dismissed to our classrooms.

Today's school went well. I am very pleased with the 10th

grade top set and in some ways wish I could stay to see them through to their exam next year, but it is just a little wish!

I was just about to do the usual battle with my 9th grade bottom set when a pupil came in to say I had to attend a meeting of senior teachers, so I had to leave the kids to amuse themselves. The meeting lasted five hours and seven minutes, I kid you not. Glory be, can these Jamaican's talk! On which topic, the Debating Club have now decided on their debate 'moot' for the next meeting. It is 'Discipline in this school is not good enough.' I know where I shall place my vote!

It is 7 p.m. and Cislyn's phone has just gone. It was to say the car is ready to collect. I'll go down tomorrow morning.

Yesterday the two officials from the Ministry, Miss Davis and Miss Jones, who greeted us on our arrival and who we met regularly in Kingston as they are in charge of teacher exchanges, were due to come out to see how I was getting on. Somewhat late in the day for their first visit seeing as I have been here a year and leave next week! They did not show on the arranged day but did arrive after our senior teaching meeting this afternoon. They were in quite a state as they had been put in fear of their lives as they drove on the road from Golden Grove. Apparently a car with three Jamaicans in it drove close behind them persistently honking its horn (remember my driving test?), then overtook them and stopped further up the road. The three Jamaicans got out and waved furiously at Miss Davis and Miss Jones.

"Do you know them Miss Davis?" said Miss Jones.

Miss Davis did not.

"Foot down, Miss Davis!!"

And they escaped.

Jamaica news has reported only this morning the murder of a French Attaché and a holidaying friend in Kingston during the night. No wonder our two ladies were frightened.

After telling us of their adventure they, Mr Symes, and I went into the Principal's office to chat. A knock on the door and a Jamaican stepped in, said "Hello" to me and shook my hand. He then started to explain to Miss Davis that he had recognised her in Golden Grove and was trying to stop her to say he was back in Jamaica. It was David! I had forgotten that Miss Davis was a teacher at the school before she landed her job at the Ministry. I don't know whose car he was in but it sure wasn't his, or more correctly that of Mr Grey. I was quite shocked at his appearance. He had a smart beard when he left for England but that was gone and he looked haggard and ill. I hope the folk in England will not think the same about me next week though I have gone quite grey myself.

Anyway David and Mr Symes soon embarked on a deep involved discussion as only Jamaicans can. They covered Britain's relationship with Europe and the ECC, Jamaican Independence, etc. etc. leaving the other three of us rather flabbergasted. Eventually Miss Davis, Miss Jones and I made our excuses and Miss Davis gave me a lift to Royal View, where they and Gemma had a chat over a cup of tea before they set off for Kingston.

And so to bed.

Love

Christopher

CHAPTER 34

Losing It

Sunday 12th April 1992

Dear Mum

Brace yourself!

Friday passed peacefully enough. David came to my classroom but wouldn't come in. The pupils did not seem to recognise him and did not react. He told me he was off to Kingston to buy four new wheels for the 'bug'. I guess his accumulated Jamaican salary must be burning a hole in his pocket. I advised him that there were far more important things to buy for the car than the wheels, which had been no trouble since I had new tyres and tubes fitted in October. Later he came into the staffroom where he asked Bob a series of demanding questions like 'What is the major difference you have noticed between the United States and Jamaica?" I don't think Bob knew where to start!

After school I caught a minibus to Port Morant to collect Horatio, soon apparently to be the proud owner of four new wheels. The minibus for once was not overcrowded with pupils as on a Friday attendance is usually only about 25%. I realise that I am defining 'not overcrowded' with a Jamaican perspective. If it was judged by British standards it would be grossly overloaded and illegal.

I got out at the repair yard, but of Horatio there was no sign. "We've managed to sell your car for you." said a young apprentice lad. A Jamaican with a keen sense of humour. Well I hoped that that was what it was. "I thought that you had exchanged it for that one." I responded, pointing to a very smart BMW that someone had brought in for a service. Much laughter all round. Anyway it turned out the mechanic had gone off to the bank while he tested the clutch repair and would probably 'cum soon'. I settled down for the second time on the old car seat balanced on an oil drum and forty-five minutes later the mechanic returned, pronouncing Horatio restored to health, fragile though that health was. Apparently it had not been possible to obtain a spare clutch lever but they had managed to repair it. I just hope the glue sticks, or at least holds on until I am well out of the country. For taking out the engine, then dismantling the clutch, repairing the lever, and putting it all back into the car the bill was only J$510. I had to ask him to repeat this twice, but that was correct. In English £12! They would charge me that to change a wiper blade in England! Anyway we parted with warm well wishes all round. "Come and say goodbye before you go!" they instructed. They are indeed good-hearted and honest Jamaicans.

Safely back home, Gemma, Bob and I went to Raj and Naomi who had cooked us a farewell meal of dahl, roti and curried fish. Naomi, like Gemma, desperately wants to leave Jamaica, though I think Raj is happy enough with his fishing (he cycles to the beach) and his use of the school workshop to construct his lovely furniture.

Yesterday morning I cleaned out Horatio, mainly sweeping up the rust, Brenda helping enthusiastically. I undertook my last weekly defrost of the fridge and removal of Cislyn's collection of stale, mildewed and rotting left overs. No wonder she gets so many gastric upsets. Then we took Camille and Brenda to Golden Grove market to say farewell to all our stallholder friends.

We had invited Bob to a late lunch, or possibly early dinner; either way Gemma got us a nutritious meal of Macaroni Cheese and Clam Chowder and the three of us had just settled down to chat when David appeared. He is an active Seventh Day Adventist so Saturday is his holy day and he had been to their service with his friend and was on his way to Port Antonio but would call in later.

At 7 p.m. David returned. I invited him into our room but he insisted on staying outside on the veranda, explaining that our room was 'a private place', which I didn't and don't understand, but supposed it must be a Jamaican convention. Bob and Gemma went in to watch the evening news. David then explained to me that, although he knew he had promised I could use his car until the day I left, he needed to visit his mother on Sunday (the next day) morning. "I'll bring it back by noon. Is that OK?"

"Yes." I said, "We can walk to church tomorrow but we have planned to visit some friends in Morant Bay in the afternoon so that works OK." I got the keys, handed them over and David left in Horatio, not without some understandable difficulty finding the light switch in the dark and sorting out the gears. He had after all only driven the car for a couple of days before he left for England.

I went to report all this to Gemma and Bob. Gemma said "You've seen the last of the car!" which I thought was cynical of her. I had David's word that the car would be back at noon the following day. Besides, when I learnt that David would be back a good week ahead of us leaving I wrote to him asking if we could still have the use of his car for the week so that we could visit friends to say our farewells. I have kept his written reply: 'No problem having the car right up to your departure hour. I am aware of your need to say last minute farewells at close range to all your friends. So go straight ahead with all your local arrangements and runs.' I thought that this was very generous of him.

Half an hour later David returned.

Clearly having become accustomed to driving my fairly new Austin Metro in England he was not prepared for Horatio's fragile constitution.

"Chris that car should not be on the road. The lights don't work. It jumps out of gear. It's a wreck. You have failed to look after it properly. It needs looking at by a proper mechanic. I am going to have to take it into a VW specialist tomorrow and you are not going to drive it again."

I am afraid I saw red at this point when I thought of all the work I had done to keep the car running throughout the year. I cannot deny that Horatio is well past her sell-by-date but is much improved compared to her sad condition when David first gave her to me. Besides, of all her many faults, the lights and the gear box were two of the few items that had always worked properly.

I am reminded of my dad reciting Stanley Holloway's 'The Lion and Albert'. Young Albert had annoyed the Lion in the zoo and the lion ate him leading to a case the the local court.

The Magistrate gave 'is opinion
That no one was really to blame
And 'e said that 'e 'oped the Ramsbottoms
Would 'ave further sons to their name
At that Mother got proper blazin':
"And thank you, sir, kindly," said she-
"Wot, spend all our lives raisin' children
To feed your ruddy lions? Not me!"

I stormed back into the room to fetch the rest of the car's documents. On my return David was outside and I rather rudely pushed them through the door grill. "You were right." I yelled at Gemma. "He is keeping the car." To Gemma's credit she did not say 'Told you so!'

Gemma, Bob and Cislyn were very concerned at me having lost my temper but eventually I calmed down and we sat there discussing the events of this bizarre evening. Having reached this far in my story of my year in Jamaica I guess you will understand what a worry the car has been almost every time we drove her but I had her in as good a condition as she had ever been all year by the time David returned.

Without transport we can see no point remaining in Duckenfield for the remaining few days so I have phoned Stanley, the previous school principal, and he is coming to fetch us once we have everything packed. We can stay with him and Fay and he will take us to the airport for our Saturday flight home. Stanley, Gemma and I are due to attend a farewell party at school on Wednesday evening, for both him (you remember he left in July) and us, which we will do.

So it is goodbye to Duckenfield and all the many wonderful kind Jamaican friends we have grown so fond of during our year here.

See you on Easter Day.

Love
Christopher

CHAPTER 35

'The Great Escape'

Tuesday 14th April 1992

Dear Mum

Here we are safely in Kingston. I have phoned Mr Symes and told him that I have lost both Horatio and my temper when David banned me from using his car as in his opinion it was not safe to drive. He is going to set up a meeting with himself, David and me to make our peace before the farewell do tomorrow. That will be good. I don't want to leave with bad feelings between us.

Today Gemma and I plan to visit for the last time the High Commission and the Ministry of Education. Fay has kindly lent me her car for the day. What a sad ending to a year that has never ceased to have another big surprise round every corner.

Cislyn was very upset at our departure yesterday. We found out what she has been up to for so many evenings recently. She has embroidered a set of tea towels illustrating a Jamaican housewife's typical week. Monday the wash, Tuesday the ironing, Wednesday the sweeping and so on to Sunday church in her Sunday best. We shall never use them, but treasure them in her memory.

Before we left we called on Mr Spencer (the cows) to say goodbye. He said "Please wait", disappeared indoors reappearing a little later in his Sunday Best (confirmation) suit so that he could wish us 'God Speed' properly. Brenda did not seem to understand that this was 'Goodbye', probably for ever, but Camille did and she was beside herself with grief. She sat on my lap, buried her head in my shoulder, and bawled until she had Gemma, Brenda and I bawling along with her.

Thursday 16th April

Our visit to the Ministry of Education on Tuesday went well. Of course we have met Miss Davis and Miss Jones many times throughout the year and become good friends. We then said our goodbye to the High Commissioner and took his wife for lunch at the lovely Devon House. She was feeling low and rather envious I think that Gemma was making her 'Great Escape'. We each had pattie and salad, followed by their wonderful. unbeatable, unforgettable, Devon House ice-cream. By one of life's eerie co-incidences 'The Great Escape' was the title of the weekend's Kingston Carnival. However, compared to what Gemma has put up with all year, our friend lives a comparitively easy lifestyle in the High Commission although she cannot avoid knowing of all the problems that exist in Jamaica not least the poverty and the hyper-inflation.

Stanley, Gemma and I set off for the farewell party yesterday afternoon and called in on Stanley's son in Morant Bay. What a home! Luxury indeed. His son owns the town's Gas Station which must be very profitable.

Mr Symes welcomed us warmly at school but the planned peace conference with David did not take place as of David there was no sign. No one at school had seen Horatio either. I hope she is OK. Stanley commented on the drive from Kingston "David cannot drive you know!" which is a bit concerning when he has had the use of my nearly new Metro all year. I guess he has taught himself as I did all those years ago.

The farewell function went well and was only an hour late starting.

The Great Escape: Kingston Carnival

Miss Davis and Miss Jones had driven over from Kingston again and have promised to come to the airport to wave us off on Saturday. There were lots of polite, nay effusive, warm and amusing things said about Stanley and then about Gemma and me. Such emotional farewells with everyone blinking back the tears. I was hugged until I was black and blue. I had no idea that they had grown so fond of us. A good job they do not know how I have been slanging them off in so many of my letters.

We were given lots of presents, many of them large, including wooden ornaments and an alabaster statue. Such generosity when they are so poorly paid and so very much appreciated, but it will mean me packing up another box to ship to England. I made a short speech which seemed to go down well. I did say I was sorry that David had not come but suggested that he was possibly stranded out in the bush with a yet-again broken down Bug, his head under the bonnet/hood as he tried to find the engine.

It is going to be so hard saying farewell to them all, not knowing if or when we shall ever meet again. Oh dear, I have come over all emotional.

Poor Jamaica. She is still suffering. The Jamaican Dollar has reached fifty to the pound, so whilst when we arrived we multiplied by seven to get a sterling equivalent we now only multiply by two. The Gleaner reports that the hospitals, including the only Mental Hospital, have no funds to buy food for their patients and will have to shut down if they do not get some funding in the next few days. However The Gleaner today reports that the International Monetary Fund have just 'kindly' loaned Jamaica another twelve million US dollars so we hope some of this will find its way to the hospitals.

More good news is that the drought has lifted over the past two days, although not in time to save Stanley, who owns several smallholdings, from losing a field of sugar cane he had planted due to the lack of water. The locals are so relieved to see the downpours, 'Blessing Rain' they call it.

Love

Christopher

CHAPTER 36

Farewell Jamaica

17th April 1992

Dear Mum

It is Good Friday or, according to Gemma, "Great Friday."

We had a pleasant relaxed day yesterday. I did some mending jobs for Fay then boxed up our farewell gifts and got them on their way to the UK. It cost me just £1.75 to send three big parcels! We called in to say farewell to Bonnie and her kittens then took our hosts out for a good dinner in a nearby restaurant.

This morning I have marked 10/1's last test and written each of them a farewell message plus letters to say goodbye to my other two classes. I have also written a thank-you to the staff for their presents and farewell do and drafted a placatory letter to David. Bob can take these for them as he is due to arrive today and will stay here overnight.

We have met such kindness everywhere we go. All too much really and I am frequently misty eyed.

18th April 1992

I am writing this in bed as we have our morning cup of tea.

Mr Symes met me on Friday as arranged in a bar in Lower Kingston. I was somewhat surprised to find him wearing just a pair of green shorts! We talked for about three hours non-stop about Jamaica, the UK and, mainly, school. He was concerned about, as he put it, the poor quality of so many of the staff, their 'indolent ways', their lack of training and planning. He told me his wife is dreading the move to 'the bush' and he is worried about his own children's education. It seemed to me he was already regretting his appointment. I explained the situation with David and how hard he found it financially to manage in England but that my school seemed pleased with his teaching. He discussed the teacher here who had been drawing a salary for doing no teaching all year. He told me she had applied for 'Eight months' study leave on full pay'. "Over my dead body!" commented Mr Symes? Altogether it made an interesting, even fascinating, last but one afternoon in Jamaica.

Bob arrived on the bus OK yesterday and cooked us an excellent aubergine bake followed by banana cake. He is clearly a talented cook. He, Stanley and Faye, Mrs White, Raj & Naomi and so many others have become very dear friends over the past months. Remind me not to do this again. The goodbyes are too painful.

The news is on as I write ...trouble, problems, strikes, killings, the falling Jamaican dollar....

And on that sombre note this is farewell from dear frustrating lovely scruffy peaceful dangerous wonderful Jamaica. God Bless Her.

See you the other side of the closing door.

Love as ever

Christopher and Gemma

Epilogue

Our flight home was trouble free and much more comfortable than anticipated as we were upgraded and had a proper bed and excellent meals with free drinks.

I hit the ground running once I had returned to Somerset as school started almost immediately. The house had thankfully been well cared for but the garden was a jungle. The Metro was fine, thank you David; sorry that you thought that I had wrecked yours.

It was Somerset County Council's turn to run out of money just two years later and I was offered an early retirement on a full pension. It took just milliseconds to decide whether to accept that or not! I did half-time supply teaching for several years and have taught maths to several hundred private pupils over the years to now.

I joined the Red Cross as a volunteer, organising our local Centre as a café and shop which provides a meeting place for many lonely pensioners. I teach first aid to adults and my team has provided first aid cover at hundreds of events.

In other words, I have been pretty busy..

It is now 2020 and the Corona/Covid19 virus has forced me into house arrest, so nearly thirty years after our adventure I have at last found that I have time on my hands to do what Bob and the League wanted me to do back in 1992, viz go through all my letters and turn them into what you have just been reading. I hope that it entertained you.

Of the folks I wrote about some have been given new names lest I cause any embarrassment. The name of our closest friends have not been changed and of these we had not seen the last of Camille, Naomi, Raj, Bob and Annie.

Gemma and I had over thirty years of married bliss until her death at nearly 83 in December 2020.

Camille did well at the High School, wrote us some

thoughtful letters, had a holiday with us in England when she was sixteen and for a few years had a job in Kingston. Then she became yet another baby-mother, lost her job and returned to live in Duckenfield. As far as we know she and her daughter are there still.

Raj landed a teaching job a few years later in Turks & Caicos Islands, a British Protectorate, and we had a great holiday there with him and Naomi. Then he got a job in a school in Norfolk and they and two of their three boys are now British Citizens, living and working in England. We remain close friends.

Bob had a holiday with us in England. I shall never forget his hysterics at seeing Spotted Dick on the pub menu on the evening of his arrival. We spent a Thanksgiving in Boston with Bob and his family, then he and Annie married and we had another lovely holiday with them in Cincinnati. I wonder if they ever reminisce about the first time they slept together!

Of the remainder of my cast:

Brenda has been financially supported by Gemma and spent two years in Antigua training to be a chef. However things do not seem to have worked out well for her and she is now living with Camille back in Duckenfield.

Cislyn we kept in touch with by letter and phone until her death in her late eighties. Gemma and I frequently used her favourite phrases, "How much?!" when we are shocked at the price of something, "What to do. What to do?" when something bad happens and we were powerless to do anything about it, and of course "It was a lovely funeral."

Stanley (first headmaster) and Fay lived well into old age, though hyper-inflation made life increasingly tough for them and Stanley's last years were marred by ill health. He also got bitten by a giant (they grow up to 25cm long) centipede and it was touch and go in a Kingston hospital for a while. I kept them well supplied with loose leaf tea for their diplomatic teapot.

David has not been in touch since he left with Horatio that evening, which is probably somewhat understandable. However Naomi met him in 2009 by a yet another fluke when she was applying at the High Commission for her UK visa to join Raj, so he too may be in the UK.

My Jamaican School benefitted from Robert's good teaching. He survived the full two years and the Years 10 and 11 exam results were the best ever. Robert also thought that Mr Symes had done a good job in sorting out many of the school's problems.

The High Commissioner and his wife managed to make their own 'Great Escape' from Jamaica in 1995 when they were posted to eastern Europe.

Horatio was, Raj thinks, soon sold on. Probably a wise move on David's part!

In case you are wondering why I have never had a driving lesson, I passed a scooter test then bought a three-wheeler car, which you could drive on a two-wheeler licence, taught myself to drive it pretty quickly(!) having nearly demolished a lamppost and finally passed my car test driving my father's four-wheeler!

Inflation continues to be a problem. The Jamaican dollar was 15 to the £1 when we arrived, 70 to the £1 when we left and today, in 2020, 170 to the £1.

The Kingston Cinema caught fire in 1997 and the interior was totally destroyed. However the exterior walls survived and in 2020 it continues to show films in the modern fashion with five mini-cinemas.

Mirrors on ceilings: When I got back to my UK school I

found a small plastic mirror had been stuck to the ceiling in my office!

The Jamaica Palace Hotel is still operating, so whoever bought it has done good. It looks as grand as when we were there. Googling it brought back some warm memories!

Kingston Zoo & Gardens: From Google it looks as if the zoo & gardens have been much improved over the past 30 years and are now a popular destination for tourists.

The League For The Exchange Of Commonwealth Teachers was founded in 1901 when of course it was for Empire teachers. It has had several transformations since 2001 but ceased arranging exchanges in 2011 when UK government funding was withdrawn. The nearest alternative that I can find is the Commonwealth Teacher Exchange Programme but this does not seem to include the Caribbean.

Ackee is sold in cans in international stores in England. It is hopefully minus the poisonous red threads but you have been warned!

Duckenfield: Google has a photo of the main street. It does not seem to have changed!

Printed in Great Britain
by Amazon